The Church:

LEARNING and TEACHING.

Ladislas Örsy, SJ

The Church:

Learning and Teaching.

Magisterium · Assent · Dissent · Academic Freedom

Michael Glazier, Inc.
Wilmington, Delaware

ACKNOWLEDGMENTS

Chapters Two and Three of this book are a revised and enlarged version of an article entitled "Magisterium: Assent and Dissent," published in *Theological Studies,* 48 (1987); reprinted here with permission.

All quotations from the Bible are from *The New Oxford Annotated Bible,* Revised Standard Version, Second Edition (New York: Oxford University Press, 1977).

All translations of the documents of Vatican Council II are taken from *Documents of Vatican II,* edited by Walter M. Abbott (New York: Herder and Herder, 1966).

First published in 1987 by Michael Glazier, Inc., 1935 West Fourth Street, Wilmington, Delaware 19805. Distributed outside the U.S., Canada and the Philippines by Dominican Publications, Dublin, and Fowler Wright Books, Leominster.

Library of Congress Catalog Card Number: 87-82812
International Standard Book Number: 0 89453 646-X (Glazier)
0 907271 83 9 (Dominican)
0 85244 140 1 (Fowler Wright)

Printed in the United States of America.

CONTENTS

ABBREVIATIONS

Abbot	*The Documents of Vatican II*
CD	*Christus Dominus.* Decree on the Bishops' Pastoral Office in the Church, Vatican II
CIC	*Codex Iuris Canonici,* 1983
DS	Denzinger and Schönmetzer, *Enchiridion Symbolorum,* ed. 34
DTC	*Dictionnaire de Théologie Catholique*
DV	*Dei Verbum.* Dogmatic Constitution on Divine Revelation, Vatican II
GS	*Gaudium et spes.* Pastoral Constitution on the Church in the Modern World, Vatican II
LG	*Lumen gentium.* Dogmatic Constitution on the Church, Vatican II
LTK	*Lexicon für Theologie und Kirche*
NCE	*New Catholic Encyclopedia*
OED	*Oxford English Dictionary*
OGD	*Oxford Greek Dictionary*
OLD	*Oxford Latin Dictionary*
UR	*Unitatis redintegratio.* Decree on Ecumenism, Vatican II

THANKS

I am grateful for the help I have received from Michael Buckley, S.J., of the Jesuit School of Theology at Berkeley, California, and from James Conn, S.J., of Fordham University, New York City. They have read the manuscript and by their questions and suggestions they have prevented me from making some mistakes and prompted me to improve my "discourse." For the final result, of course, I alone am responsible.

Further, I wish to thank Michael Glazier; without his firm judgment and gentle perseverance this book would not have seen the light.

Finally, I am indebted to the Jesuit Community at Fordham University: through their generous hospitality they gave me the opportunity to read, reflect and write.

PROLOGUE

"I have yet many things to say to you, but you cannot bear them now. When the Spirit of truth comes, he will guide you into all the truth..."

(John 16:12-13)

This book is about the whole church, learning and teaching, and about the journey of the faithful toward the fullness of the truth.

The whole community is the church learning. Their teacher is the Spirit of truth who reveals them the Word of God and guides them through the vicissitudes of human history.

The whole community is the church teaching. They all are called to proclaim the Word and bring testimony to its truth—who could deny that this is teaching in the best sense of the term?

God has so ordered in his providence that some among the faithful should be chosen to be "servants of the the servants of God" (a title first used by Pope Gregory the

Great): they are the bishops, presided over by the bishop of Rome. Their task is to be the keepers of God's own household (an ancient description of their office); in particular they have a special ministry in sanctifying the community in truth (cf. John 17:17).

Overall the book speaks about the slow, joyful and painful progress of the community toward "all the truth"; a journey marked with lights and shadows. It is also a journey which through the fidelity of the Spirit leads unerringly into the fullness of the light.

Procedamus in pace, in nomine Domini: let us go forward in peace, in the name of the Lord.

1

FOUNDATIONS AND CONTEXT

The fundamental theme of this book is the progress of the Christian community toward the whole truth.[1] It is about the Word of God that was given to the church, and about the interplay that takes place between those who possess the Word (that is, the whole church) and those who within that community have a special power to proclaim it and authenticate it (that is, the episcopate[2]).

[1] In this book the footnotes play a more important role than is usual. They contain further explanations on the main topics, also some asides, *obiter dicta*, which may enliven an otherwise heavy subject matter and bring some relief to the reader who is asked to traverse an unfamiliar territory. My aim was to safeguard the unity of exposition in the main text while providing some more information and a few diversions in the footnotes.

Bibliographical references in the footnotes are given in full only when a work referred to is not listed in the main Bibliography.

[2] "Episcopate" throughout this study means the episcopal college in the sense that it is described and explained in Chapter Three of *Lumen gentium*.

The college is an organic social body, which has for its head the pope, and for its other members the bishops. Unless the body is *whole*, that is, the

This should not be taken as if the church were divided into two separate groups. All have received the Word, but some among them were given the sacramental mandate to speak it with authority and, should dissensions arise in the community, to determine its true meaning with unfailing fidelity.

About this interplay many questions are raised today. In

head and the other members are working together, there is no college.

"Conciliarism" is false because it assumes that a body without its head can be a living body. On the other hand, a head that would try to operate independently of the other members, could harm the body in many ways.

The body is held together by *communio* among all the members. The church is at its healthiest when there is a steady and vigorous exchange among all the members.

There has been a great deal of discussion at the Council and immediately after about the position of the pope. Some held that he had two offices: he was the Vicar of Christ (strictly personal) *and* the head of the college (collegial). This meant that if something went wrong with the college presided over by him (e.g., at a council), he could (as it were) step outside of it and correct it as Vicar of Christ. The so called *Nota praevia* undoubtedly reflects this view. Others held that the pope had one office: he was the head of the college.

The first opinion appears highly artificial and unnecessarily complicated (a theory must not postulate more than what is necessary to explain the facts); the second one is much more in harmony with the organic nature of the church. There is no need to assume that the pope must step outside of a council to correct its course, should it ever be necessary; he can do it just as well, or better, from the inside, as its head. See Granfield, *The Limits of the Papacy,* pp. 77-106.

There are also problems with the title "Vicar of Christ"; the Council applied it to every diocesan bishop. A more traditional title for the pope is "Vicar of Peter"; see Tillard, *The Bishop of Rome,* pp. 92-100.

particular, people want to know more concerning the role and extent of the "teaching power" in the church, and their obligations in responding to its voice.

All questions about this authority converge directly on some fundamental concepts, such as magisterium, which can be exercised either in a solemn or in an ordinary manner, and which can be either infallible or non-infallible. Similarly, the questions concerning the obligations to respond lead immediately to the concepts of assent and dissent. Ordinarily this response is a matter of conscience for individual persons, yet it can also involve deeply an institution which is called the "house of the intellect": the university.

The scope and purpose of this essay (because an essay it is in the classical sense of the term[3]) is to clarify some of these foundational concepts and to present a framework in which the interplay between the teaching authority and the whole community can be understood. Once we have an understanding of the internal dynamics of this interplay and of the external structures in which it takes place, we

[3]See in the *New Columbia Encyclopedia*, p. 892:

> **essay**, relatively short literary composition in prose, in which a writer discusses a topic, usually restricted in scope, or tries to persuade the reader to accept a particular point of view.
>
> A fitting definition in this case, perhaps even for the "trying to persuade" part of it; if, however, an attempt to persuade is present in the text, it should be in the internal cohesion and harmony of the ideas proposed, and not in any kind of rhetoric!

are in a better position to make prudent decisions and move on to wise actions.

The literary form of this essay can be best described as a reflective piece, a "theological discourse", built on foundations which are mostly taken for granted here.[4] There is a season for gathering informational data, there is another for reflecting on them in order to understand them, and there is one again for formulating practical policies on the basis of the understanding achieved. I shall certainly use informational data, but my main scope will be to reflect on them, with a view to finding good norms for action. Faith seeks understanding; indeed, but faith seeks action also. St. Anselm of Canterbury, I am sure, would not object to such an extension of his dictum.

The field we enter and intend to explore presents us with varied situations. There are things which we know and understand quite well, although the cohesion among them may not have been brought to light fully. There are

---

[4]My intention is *not* to present comprehensive and systematic treatments of the topics discussed in this book; there are such works available. Nor do I wish to repeat what has been handled with some detail in other publications, not even if they are of importance, e.g. the statement by the International Theological Commission in 1975; there is a thorough review of it in Sullivan's *Magisterium*, pp. 174-217.

"Notes and Reflections" or "Meditations" would not have been misleading subtitles for this "discourse."

other things which we do not know fully. They keep us puzzled; still, we know enough about them to raise some good questions, even if we cannot produce satisfactory answers. And (a reasonable presumption!) there must be hidden things or events, which we have not even noticed, let alone raised questions about!

Socrates spent a life trying to find out how much he did not know; worse still, he tried to demonstrate to his fellow citizens how much they did not know! He practiced his art of questioning relentlessly, and he found it helped him to grow in wisdom. It was an unusual (and as it turned out, dangerous!) enterprise in fifth century Athens, and he paid a terrible price for it.

One wonders if a courageous soul should not attempt a similar venture in the field of our contemporary theology, since we may have reached a point where affirmations abound and are pitted against each other in great intellectual battles but little is said about "what we do not know." This is all the more surprising given the fact that the proper subject matter of theology is mysteries, which by definition defeat our effort to know.

Admittedly, in sciences which deal with the human spirit (*Geisteswissenschaften,* as the Germans incisively call them), it is always easier to claim certainty than in sciences which deal with inanimate matter. After all, if a physicist or chemist is wrong in his assumptions, there is a built-in penalty: his experiment may end in disaster and his equipment may be blown into pieces.[5] No such thing ever happens in the field of philosophy or theology; it may take generations before the collective and corrective forces of critical reviews can have their impact.

Be that as it may, the time for a *Summa* on What-we-do-not-know may not have come yet. Nor has a godly Socrates appeared in our market places to teach us *his* kind of wisdom. Let us proceed therefore as we can: with some affirmations (when there are good grounds to support them), with some questions (when we know enough to put them correctly), and with the hope that we might even expand (a little) our horizons into the hitherto unknown.

---

[5]No one knew this better than Einstein who experienced both successes and failures in building scientific theories:

> The scientific theorist is not to be envied. For Nature, or more precisely experiment, is an inexorable and not very friendly judge of his work. It never says "Yes" to a theory. In the most favorable cases it says "Maybe," and in the great majority of cases simply "No." If an experiment agrees with a theory it means for the latter "Maybe," and if it does not agree it means "No.". Probably every theory will someday experience its "No" - most theories soon after conception.

(Quoted in Julian Schwinger, *Einstein's Legacy*, [New York: Scientific American Library, 1986] p. 203.)

This built-in control by mother nature is not present in the theological enterprise.

A preliminary note on the historical context

It may well be that a future historian of Christian doctrine will describe our times (from the second part of the nineteenth century onward) as the age when the church was coming to grips with the laws of evolution, especially in doctrinal matters.[6]

[6] The reluctance (or struggle) to accept evolution as a fact of life marks the official attitude of the church on a much broader scale than in reference to doctrinal issues only. The reasons for this are probably manifold. There is the instinct to preserve our ancient traditions, and any potential change is easily perceived as a dangerous step toward infidelity. Also, in the Western church at least, our traditions have been explained in Aristotelian-Thomistic categories, which are not attuned to an evolving universe. Further, in official literature the sayings and actions of the church have been presented, more often than it was necessary or justified, as being of the highest degree of wisdom and prudence; hence no room was left for improvements.

Even in the recently (1983) promulgated Code of Canon Law, there are no provisions for a peaceful and ordered development of ecclesiastical laws and structures (that is, laws and structures of human origin, therefore historically conditioned); although the need for such provisions in a community which is alive, growing and serving the needs of the human family, is fairly obvious.

The absence of orderly procedures is one of the reasons why the Catholic Church suffers so frequently from internal agitations and conflicts; they appear to the faithful as the only means of bringing to the notice of the authorities that some measure of change is needed.

In fairness, the Dogmatic Constitution on Divine Revelation, *Verbum Dei*, of Vatican Council II, has done much to correct the situation. It proclaims that continuity and change go hand in hand in the church. But there is a long way from the clarity of intellectual insights to the revision of practical attitudes and the creation of new structures.

Not that there has not been some awareness of evolution before; there has been. No one at the Council of Nicaea (325) thought that the term *homoousios* was in the Scriptures, nor did anyone at the Council of Trent (1545-63) pretend that a specific enumeration of the seven sacraments could be found in the Bible. But there was not (not until Newman, that is) any competent analysis of the phenomenon of the development of doctrine; there was no reliable theory to explain its mysterious process.[7]

It took a long time, however, for Newman's insights, to be accepted. But the fact of doctrinal development could not be discarded; in one way or another the issue kept returning. Questions that the church could not ignore kept arising. Was the universe really created in six days, according to the pattern described in Genesis, or did it evolve over so many billions of years, as the scientists argued? Did Moses himself write the Pentateuch, or is it a document that matured over several centuries? Have the four gospels been conceived independently from each other, or are they the fruits of protracted reflections on the earliest common traditions? And so forth . . . Today, we may well know how to respond to these questions, but when they were first mooted, the answers were not readily

[7]There is no better work in English on the development of doctrine than Jan Hendrik Walgrave, *Unfolding Revelation: The Nature of Doctrinal Development*, translated from the Dutch. There is no more comprehensive work on the same subject than George Söll, *Dogma und Dogmenentwicklung*, in German.

available and there was a great turmoil in our household.[8] Moreover, as natural sciences developed, humanity became confronted with moral problems about which the church could not remain indifferent. Yet, there were no obvious solutions in the treasury of our ancient traditions, unless, of course, the traditions themselves could evolve and bring forth responses old *and new!* The questions kept multiplying: Could a healthy person donate one of his kidneys to his brother who needs it to survive? Are atomic

[8]Decree of the Biblical Commission, 27 June 1906:

> *Question:* Are the arguments, adduced by critical authors to attack the authentic authorship of Moses of the sacred books, known under the name of Pentateuch, of such weight that they give the right to affirm that Moses is not the author of the books; notwithstanding the testimony of the Old and New Testaments, the perpetual consensus of the Jewish people, the permanent tradition of the church, the internal evidence present in the text itself . . .?
>
> *Answer:* Negative.
>
> *Question:* Does the authentic authorship of Moses require us to hold that he wrote each of the books with his own hands, or dictated each to scribes, or, can another hypothesis be permitted, namely which holds that after he conceived his work under divine inspiration, he committed it to one or several persons to write it down, with the provision that they had to preserve the original sense faithfully, write nothing against his will, omit nothing; and finally when the work was completed, the work was to be published in his name?
>
> *Answer:* Negative for the first part; positive for the second part.

Approved by the Supreme Pontiff: 27 June 1906. (See DS 3394, 3395)

weapons acceptable for legitimate self-defense? Is fertilization *in vitro* permissible? What is the right balance between the public good and the private ownership of goods? And so on . . . [9]

To find the correct answers, it was not enough to come to an understanding of the *abstract concept* of the development of doctrine; it was also necessary to understand that the *concrete reality* of the church was subject to evolution. Such new perceptions were not always well received; they seemed to conflict with the permanency of the word of God and the stability of the institution.

In the long and complex struggle which ensued, the need for clarifying some key concepts emerged; a need that is still with us. What is the correct meaning of magisterium? What is the difference between doctrine taught infallibly and doctrine not so taught? Can a line be drawn between the two, or do they form an organic and undivided unity?

[9]Each age in Christian history has its own interest. The great disputes in the early centuries were about the internal life of God (Father, Son and Holy Spirit: one God) and his communication with the created universe (the Son became flesh); the focus of the attention of the church was the very core, heart, or center of revelation.

Today disputes on morality tend to override all other interests. Important as moral issues may be, if in the mind of the people they overshadow the great mysteries of the Trinity and of the Incarnation, and of the "divinization" of human persons. A slanted perception of the good news emerges—which news may not even appear all that good since not enough attention is paid to the very best of the message. Once this happens, the religious life of the believers becomes impoverished and the evangelization of the unbelievers becomes difficult.

What is the *obsequium* due to the non-infallible teaching of the magisterium? How far is dissent allowed?[10]

This process of clarification has by no means been concluded; it is going on. The final answers are not in the consciousness of the church - whether we like to admit it or not. To be in such a predicament is rather humiliating for an otherwise infallible community; but in truth, to search for the whole truth, with all the fallibility that such a search may entail, belongs to the humanity of the church.[11]

[10]There is a remote parallel between developments in philosophical and theological thinking. Ever since Kant, much effort in philosophical reflection has been expended on understanding the operations of the mind and the process of knowing. Ever since Newman, much effort in the Catholic Church has been put into discovering and understanding the process of perceiving and articulating the data of revelation—reflections on how the mind of the church operates and how some knowledge of the mysteries is achieved.

[11]Much has been written and said about the divine gifts with which God has endowed his church; no one described them better than Vatican Council II in the Dogmatic Constitution of the Church, *Lumen gentium*. But councils, popes, bishops and theologians, as a rule shied away from speaking of, and reflecting on, the humanity of the church. The result is that we are often unaware of the limitations and shortcomings that flow from this humanity; we tend to deny them; we act as if they did not exist; we take no precautions and protections against them. But an imbalance in the perception of any reality, even if that reality is part of the church, can lead to disaster in the practical order.

The preaching or teaching of the theology of the church according to *Lumen gentium* must be always balanced by a parallel course on church history.

While the church cannot fail in proclaiming the evangelical message, the charism of sudden enlightenment in resolving issues has never been promised to Peter, or to the twelve, or to any of their successors.[12] Consequently, those who have authority need time to study the new problems, to come to grips with them, and to reach conclusions grounded in faith and reason. Important as a question may be, a final and authentic answer may not be easily and quickly available.[13]

This apparent vagueness and slowness can be disappointing all the more now that we have become used to clarity and to speedy solutions. Scholastic philosophy and theology taught us about a well ordered universe, natural and supernatural, where all things and all beings can be defined by *genus* and *species;* it taught us order and clarity.

Moreover, right before our eyes, modern technology is providing instantaneous answers to problems which (as we kept thinking) were beyond the power of the human mind; it taught us to expect speedy solutions. It is only natural that we build up similar expectations toward the operations of the church: we want clear answers without delay; we want to see scholastic orderliness produced with

[12]One needs to remember how slow the apostles were in understanding the message of Jesus—as it is recorded in the gospels.

[13]An intemperate zeal in pressing for an answer can do more harm than good. Those in authority ought to resist such pressure; at times the honest answer can be only "As yet, we do not know!"

computerized efficiency.[14] But that is not how our church lives and operates.[15]

The pattern of the encounter between God and human persons

The interplay between the acts of the teaching authority and the response of the community takes place in a broad

[14]Aristotle taught the Latin theologians to be relentless in their inquiries. Thus, the scholastics wanted to know the exact moment when the bread became the body of Christ, and the significance of the words of consecration was stressed without giving an equal importance to the unity of the eucharistic prayer, including the invocation of the Holy Spirit. Or, the canonists wanted to know the precise moment when marriage came into existence; once determined, all validity had to turn on the disposition of the parties at that point of time, with little possibility left for the healing of an initial defect. Divine mysteries are not like physical bodies: to have some understanding of them, we must keep a respectful distance.

[15]I recall that a favorite saying of Yves Congar during the Council was that a safeguard for the church in the course of history is in examining itself regularly "in the mirror of the Gospel." My own reflections: The Gospel does not show a neatly organized and efficiently run community. But it displays a belief that the Spirit takes care of the group of believers. In fact, several of the images and parables present the church as a rather "mixed" gathering: it is like a field where good and bad plants grow side by side until the harvest; it is like a haul of fish with creatures good and bad in the net; it is like a flock where some of the sheep have gone astray but still belong to it, . . . and so forth.

I am not suggesting that we should not try to be efficient; there are many parables about provident administrators as well. But at times the desire for order and clarity can go beyond the evangelical limits.

context: it is part of an on-going communication between the Creator and his creatures. To see this broader picture will help us to achieve a better understanding of the interplay we are interested in.[16]

1. God touches the heart.

Any first encounter between God and human persons happens in the depth of the human spirit, without words and without signs. The Spirit of God reaches out for human beings, who in a gentle and mysterious way are invited to surrender to God. In this encounter the first promptings toward faith are perceived, the initial stirrings of hope are experienced, and an invitation to love a transcendental being is sensed. Such communications are inarticulate (ineffable would be a better word), but no less

---

[16]What we describe here is certainly of scriptural inspiration. The passages which affirm that it is the Spirit who moves a person to surrender to God in faith are too numerous to be quoted; also, the passages which say that the Spirit is the one who helps the hearer to recognize the truth in the message of the preacher, are frequent, too.

Much effort has been expended by theologians to organize the scriptural data into a cohesive system. Some of the more recent ones who should be mentioned are Pierre Rousselot (1878-1915) among the French; he spoke of the "eyes of faith," *les yeux de la foi*, better translated "the eyes that faith gives"; Karl Rahner among the Germans who insisted on the openness of our human nature to the infinite, hence to the transcendental gift of grace; Bernard Lonergan who taught in Rome but did much of his work in Canada and spoke of a "conversion" at the invitation of the Spirit and of "belief" in accepting the message.

real for that. They are not (as yet) bound to any profession of faith. They may happen to anybody (we believe that it does happen to everybody), independently from what a person may or may not know in a conceptual way about God.

This initial encounter is the first stage in a dynamic pattern, which is meant to continue, for the simple reason that God lives and wants to communicate with his creatures.

> At this level the teaching authority has no role to play; no more need be said.

2. *God speaks.*

In the second stage of his encounter with human beings God speaks. He speaks externally, using the language of those to whom he has chosen to speak; words, sentences, signs—anything through which a meaning can be conveyed.[17] This communication reached its peak when

[17]In the Hebrew tradition God appears right from the beginning as the "Speaking God." With his Word he creates the universe; he keeps talking to his creatures in and out of the garden of Eden; he instructs Noah; he calls Abraham and keeps conversing with him as a friend; he appoints Moses to lead his people out of Egypt; he never ceases to communicate with his prophets; and then

> in these last days he has spoken to us by a Son, whom he appointed the heir of all things, through whom also he created the world. He reflects the glory of God and bears the very stamp of his nature, upholding the universe by his word of power.
>
> (Heb. 1:2-3)

the *Logos*, the eternal word of God, "was made flesh" and proclaimed the coming of the Kingdom and the universal call to salvation. This proclamation was in a language that we could understand, as that mystery

> which was not made known to the sons of men in other generations as it has now been revealed to his holy apostles and prophets by the Spirit . . .
> (Eph. 3:5)

But no matter how close God may be to his creatures and what language he may be using, if he speaks about his mysteries, there is a problem in communication: the truth of his speech cannot be tested by our ordinary criteria; the proofs we can handle do not reach up to his mysteries.[18]

We Christians believe that God has appointed the church (the whole church) to continue to speak his Word by proclaiming to all nations the good news of salvation, and also by speaking with power in the sacraments the word of sanctification. (It is interesting to note that the most powerful word of sanctification is spoken in baptism, which brings a participation in the divine nature and gives a capacity for other sacraments, and that *this powerful word can be spoken by every Christian.*)

[18]It should not really surprise us that there is such a problem, after all

> as the heavens are higher than the earth, so are my ways higher than your ways and my thoughts than your thoughts [*says the Lord*] (Is. 55:9)

—and that is the problem: there is a gap; and it cannot be bridged by the operations of our mind.

He may well be speaking, but how can we know that he is the speaker; how can we know that the content of the speech we hear is true?

The Spirit of God it is who comes to our rescue:

> . . . no one comprehends the thoughts of God except the Spirit of God. Now we have received not the spirit of the world, but the Spirit which is from God, that we might understand the gifts bestowed on us by God. (1 Cor. 2, 11-12)

That is, the gap is bridged by the Spirit. He does it by lifting up our minds and hearts to recognize the one who speaks, to understand his speech and then to surrender to the truth of what he says. We accept what we hear externally on the testimony which we perceive internally. The acceptance is not the fruit of logically compelling proofs. Paul's words are to the point:

> Therefore I want you to understand that no one speaking by the Spirit of God ever says "Jesus be cursed!" and no one can say "Jesus is the Lord" except by the Holy Spirit. (1 Cor. 12:3)

To conclude: when someone says, "Jesus is the Lord" the encounter is completed; the first and the second stage blend into one. The closing act is a profession of faith.

> At this stage, the specific role of the episcopate, which is the teaching authority, is to bring witness to the word that God has spoken; nothing more, nothing less.

> The Spirit assists them (protects them) in such a way that in their collective and solemn declarations they cannot bring false testimony to the Word. Through their ministry the scope and purpose of the Incarnation is safeguarded, the Word once proclaimed cannot be lost in the vagaries of history or among the passions of human minds.

3. *Faith seeks understanding.*

The interplay (a sacred play) does not end there: faith seeks understanding. The mind that receives the Word is not satisfied with simply repeating it, but with a steady effort will seek to penetrate it deeper and deeper. There the work of systematic theological reflection starts. Indeed, the beginnings of it are already in the Scriptures: the prophets reflected on Yahweh's words and deeds and tried to explain their fuller meaning to the people. In the New Testament, there is no piece that does not carry some reflections on the events of Jesus's life and his words; such reflections abound especially in the writings of Paul and John.

Indeed, ever since the beginning of Christian times, the faithful and the church did not cease to meditate on the events of our redemption and on the meaning of the saving message we have heard. Insight followed insight, and they were expressed in the writings of the great Fathers of the church in the early centuries, in the voluminous disputations of the scholastic theologians in the middle ages, and in the penetrating reflections of outstanding thinkers in the nineteenth and twentieth centuries. Faith was seeking understanding, and the church has become immensely enriched in the intelligence of faith.

Faith seeking understanding is again a part in the dynamic process of the encounter between God and human beings; a stage which can never exist separately, it is the fruit of the earlier ones and leads also to another one. Therefore, to draw too sharp a line between these "stages" would be wrong; they flow from, and into, each other; they compenetrate to some degree; they form an organic unity. Yet, each retains its distinctive character within the whole.

> The role of the teaching authority at this stage is different because the emphasis is not any more on witnessing the truth but on penetrating deeper into its meaning in a systematic way. To this all are called who are in possession of the revelation. It is an activity sustained by the Spirit, but feeding also from human ingenuity. Besides, while there is a simplicity in witnessing the truth and surrendering to it, at this stage the complexities and sophistication of human thought patterns play an increasing role. Some of the early Fathers approached revelation with Platonic images and ideas; the scholastic theologians borrowed their thought pattern from Aristotle; more recent theologians reached out for fresh methods and new categories into the world of modern philosophers; dispersed seeds of truth can be found in unexpected places! The episcopate has this capacity of seeking a systematic understanding

as much as the rest of the faithful (in God's Providence can have it even more), but it is not the specific charism conferred on the bishops at their ordination. Hence, there is no divine guarantee that at any given moment of history the bishops have the deepest insights into the divine mysteries.

4. Faith seeks action.

The interplay (or sacred play) continues: faith is seeking action. Human persons cannot grow unless they move from thoughts to deeds; human communities cannot develop unless they reach out for values and make them their own. Jesus himself spoke of his ministry of preaching and teaching as the sowing of the good seed destined to bear fruit—a hundredfold. The fruit of the Word received is in godly deeds.

> The episcopate has the power to guide the church toward the fullness of the kingdom. It has also the role to proclaim the basic Christian values which the faithful, individual persons and communities, must seek. Also, it is called to uphold basic human values which the "eyes of faith" can perceive. But there could be complex issues of morality about which "witnessing" in the ordinary sense is difficult to the point of being nearly impossible because the revelation is silent about them.
>
> Further, in ordering the practical life of the church, all kinds of human considerations can enter into the

decisions and actions of those who have authority; considerations which do not come from the Spirit.

*

With this, I conclude this all too brief presentation of the pattern of the encounter that takes place between God and human beings. A description of the whole process was necessary in order to understand each part in it and appreciate the various roles that different members of the community can play in it. But some particular questions still need further clarifications.

Who is in possession of the Word?

A fundamental question, surely, is: who is in possession of the Word of God? In other terms: to whom has God spoken, and to whom has he entrusted his Word? Did he give it to the episcopate so that they alone have it and they alone can communicate it to others? Or did he give it to each one of the faithful so that he or she can form the ultimate judgement on the authenticity of the Word? Or did he give it to the people as a collectivity so that they speak it authentically with the voice of the majority?

The answer is that he has spoken to the whole church, and that he has entrusted his Word to the whole church. But this was not like the depositing of a document for safekeeping; a document in which there is no life and which must be kept unaltered forever.

The whole church is in possession of revelation. But (as it were) God had to provide for two necessities: let the church grow in the understanding of the Word, but also, let the Word be safeguarded in this process. The "growing into" the Word is surely the task of the whole church, of each and all, bishops and laity. The formal safeguarding of it, however, is part of the sacramental ministry of the episcopate. Sacramental is a key word here: they can do it in virtue of a power received through ordination, independently of their merits.

Thus, the interplay is not between two separate or opposed parts of the church, the bishops *versus* their subjects; it is more subtle: all participate in one vital development but to some of them is given the charism to prevent the others from going in a wrong direction.

We are now in position to handle the next question.

What does it mean to speak the Word with authenticity?

In theological literature, there is a permanent problem with the meaning of the word "authentic" and its derivatives. If anything the problem is compounded in canon law. The ambivalence inherent in the term is brought out in the listing of the *Oxford English Dictionary*: "authentic" can mean "of authority, . . . entitled to obedience or respect," or "really proceeding from its reputed source or author, of undisputed origin, genuine." Those meanings are not the same; the first one can be rendered also as "official," the second one must be rendered as "genuine."

Vatican Council II uses the word repeatedly—but not univocally: bishops are "authentic teachers" (LG 25), the pope has an "authentic teaching authority . . . even when he is not speaking ex cathedra" (LG 25), and "the task of authentically interpreting the word of God . . . has been entrusted exclusively to the living teaching office of the church" (DV 10). The word is the same, but the meaning keeps shifting. At one time, what is authentic is not necessarily infallible (therefore fallible); at another time, authentic implies utter fidelity to the word of God (which is equivalent to being infallible.)

The same ambivalence is found in the new Code of Canon Law. Canon 753 uses the term authentic with the warning that it may be compatible with error:

> The bishops . . . although not endowed with infallibility in teaching, are authentic doctors and teachers of the faith for the faithful entrusted to their care. . .

Canon 749 uses the same word to designate infallibility:

> The College of Bishops is also endowed with infallibility in teaching . . . whenever the bishops gathered in an ecumenical council . . . or whenever, dispersed in the

whole world, . . . they authentically teach what belongs to faith and morals, . . . as to be definitively held.

The conclusion is inevitable: the official documents of the church use the term "authentic" in two distinct senses; the one is "official but subject to correction if so warranted"; the other is "really proceeding from its reputed source or author, of undisputed origin, genuine."[19]

Thus, there are two types of authentic teaching; one with authority but not irreformable; the other with the assistance of the Spirit solemnly confirming that a particular point of doctrine is an integral part of God's revelation. The capacity for such an authentication (in the fullest sense), the Catholic church believes, is given to the episcopal college.

The Word, therefore, cannot get lost; after nearly two thousand years, I can still hear the message. If there were no ways and means of finding it with certainty today, as far as I am concerned, the preaching of the *Logos* would have been in vain. His words would have been an ephemeral phenomenon, long lost in the mist of history.

Of course, it would be useless to search in the New Testament for an explicit statement concerning the power of the episcopate to authenticate the Word; it has developed gradually. Originally, the apostles were given

[19]On the use of "authentic" see also the judicious remarks of Sullivan in his *Magisterium*, pp. 26-28.

the command to go out and proclaim the mighty deeds of God; they carried the genuine Word; they witnessed what they had seen and heard; *they* were the link between Jesus and the first converts. But what about later generations? How could they know?

Long before a theoretical answer was worked out, the church found a practical solution, and found it in an existential way. If there were dissensions, peace and unity had to be restored; a decision had to be made. Thus, from the earliest of times, the practice of holding synods developed. The deliberations and the decisions of the first one are reported in the Acts of the Apostles (concerning the observance of Judaic laws by converts from paganism; see Acts 15). Eventually, the local synods led to "great synods"—we call them ecumenical councils. Behind this evolution, there was, no doubt, the conviction that the Spirit of the Lord would always be with the community, and protect it from falsehood. But if the synods could mislead the church, there would be no protection—which was unthinkable.

Out of such existential considerations, the doctrine of the "assistance" of the Spirit developed. This doctrine is of great finesse. It sees the Spirit as giving life to the church, nourishing it, sheltering it and protecting it, and in particular preventing the universal episcopate from misleading it through a false proclamation. For the sake of the chosen ones, the Spirit does not allow corruption to penetrate into the evangelical message.[20]

This assistance of the Spirit must not be conceived as something magical, coming instantaneously (whispering words to inspire a statement) or working dramatically (striking down someone to prevent a fatal error). No. The best way of understanding it, or to have a good image representing it, is to think of *Christos Pantocrator,* Christ to whom all power was given in heaven and earth, who takes care of his church. In his providence, which extends from the beginning of all times to their very end, he orders all things in such a way that his church will be preserved in truth through the ministry of those whom he chooses to follow the early witnesses. It is a gentle way of providing, through the invisible work of the Spirit, independently from any human merit, by ordering the succession of events to a goal that was set by God. Our faith is ultimately not in any bishop or pope but in the *Christos Pantocrator* who is intent to keep his Word alive in the church.[21]

[20]To put it differently: Christ sent the apostles to be witnesses to the fact of the resurrection. But today there are no such living witnesses to the same event. How do I know? I accept the Word of the church because the Spirit witnesses in my heart that it is the truth (the evidence is from the Spirit, not from anyone else). At the same time the Spirit protects those who have taken the place of the apostles from misleading me in narrating the truth.

[21](We believe that:) The One who holds this world in his hands and has so arranged the course of human events that Simon and Andrew, James and John should meet him at his own appointed time by the Sea of Galilee, is also taking care of his church in such a way that the right persons are

What is the meaning of the distinction between the teaching church and the church taught, ecclesia docens and ecclesia discens?

Its correct meaning is certainly not that there are two distinct groups of Christians, one doing the instructing, the other the learning. The whole church, no one excepted, is a learning church. There is no person who does not have the invitation (and duty!) to learn more and more about the word of God. Who could ever claim that he or she does not need to progress toward the whole truth? Moreover, who could ever claim that Christians of past or present generations could not teach him new insights or greater wisdom?

We all belong to the learning church.

The whole church, each and every one in it, is called also to proclaim the Word. In fact, this is what is happening: mothers are instructing their children, catechists are explaining the message, missionaries are spreading the Word the world over. *They are teaching.* One could even go further: during Vatican Council II theologians were instructing bishops, very much so. On many evenings

always around, at an appointed time and place, to prevent the universal church from falling victim to false beliefs.

Our belief in the proclamations of an ecumenical councils is ultimately belief in a provident God who is both firm and gentle in carrying out his plans: *disponens omnia firmiter et suaviter.*

when conferences were held all over the city of Rome, the authentic teachers of the church were genuine learners. On the next morning it may have been the bishops' turn; they approved of the documents which were meant to instruct the whole church, theologians included.

What then can this distinction mean? It can have a meaning in certain well defined circumstances. When an ecumenical council solemnly proclaims the Catholic doctrine, it teaches in the name of the whole church; and the rest of the church is being taught. But the process does not end there: often those who are so taught are able to find a deeper meaning in the doctrine proclaimed than the proclaimers themselves.[22] Many bishops who with their votes contributed to the decisions of Vatican Council II have greatly benefited from reading later the commentaries of theologians. Thus the learners became teachers, and the teachers became learners. In this way the church progresses toward the whole truth.

If the church is healthy and vigorous, there will be a strong and creative interplay between the various members and groups, each contributing according to their calling and capacity to the work of proclaiming the good news. If,

[22]Newman's writings testify that he probably (certainly?) achieved a better *understanding* (*intel-legere*) of the doctrine of infallibility than many of the bishops who defined it at Vatican Council I—including the bishop of Rome, Pius IX. The bishops had the capacity to bear authentic witness to the existence of the mystery, the theologian had the charism to penetrate its meaning to a depth that eventually was universally appreciated.

however, some members or groups ("constituents") of the church are less than able to make their own contribution, there will be a vacuum and a shift; others will take their place. Thus, if there is no laity, well informed, reflective and articulate in speech, the clergy will take over, and will begin to function as if they were the only teachers, or the only thinkers, and so forth. The so called "clericalization" of the life of the church was probably brought upon us by such a vacuum and consequent shift. Admittedly, the situation is now changing: ever since Vatican Council II a better balance has been sought and there is a gradual progress (even if unduly slow) in granting to the laity their rightful inheritance.

Is there a cultural change affecting the interplay between the episcopate and rest of the community?

Yes, an immensely great cultural change is taking place, and is making its impact felt on the exercise of magisterium and on the response of the people to the teaching authority. This cultural change is in the steadily rising educational level of the Christian people, clergy and laity.

No one should say that this development is on a purely natural level, therefore it cannot affect the exercise of a supernatural office. Rarely does the episcopal college, rarely does the pope as its head, proclaim solemnly with full apostolic authority an article of faith. Most of the time, their magisterium consists in "official" teaching but with less finality, which means that there can be many human elements entering into their declarations. In such teaching situations, the educational level of the community matters a great deal. A well informed laity can direct the attention of the episcopate to current problems, they can help the bishops to formulate the questions correctly before an answer is attempted; more importantly, when the official response is given, they can evaluate it.[23]

[23]To describe the task of the laity as *primarily and principally* secular is erroneous. Before anyone can have a lay or clerical vocation, each has a Christian vocation through the sacrament of baptism. This is a vocation to the sacred. Vatican Council II was very explicit about this:

> The laity are gathered together in the People of God and make up the Body of Christ under one Head. Whoever they are, they are called upon, as living members, to expend all their energy for the growth of the Church and its continuous sanctification. For this very energy is a gift of the Creator and a blessing of the Redeemer.
> The lay apostolate, however, is a participation in the saving mission of the Church itself. Through their baptism and confirmation, all are commissioned to that apostolate by the Lord Himself. (LG 33)

I wonder if there is not an imbalance in our theology of the sacraments. Mainly for historical reasons, too much attention has been given to the sacrament of order and not enough to the sacrament of baptism. Order is rooted in baptism, and no matter how extensively we are able to discourse on order, as long as our understanding of baptism lacks depth and breadth, our understanding of order will suffer too. A visible proof of this imbalance is that in our contemporary church there is an overabundant symbolism in clothing, titles, speech in connection with the sacrament of order, virtually

Admittedly, not all over the world has the educational level risen, but it cannot be denied that in most places it is rising, and in some places has already reached a very high level.

If the magisterium is not aware of this radical change, and continues to speak and act as if the majority of Christian people had no higher education, and no theological training, surprisingly sharp conflicts may emerge. Reasonable and responsible proposals from the laity and clergy will be regarded as uncalled-for meddling. This in its turn may cause resentment and anger. Official declarations may be supported with arguments which do not satisfy the critically well trained mind. Then the magisterium may simply appeal to a divine authority, when it is common knowledge that the matter has not

nothing in connection with the sacrament of baptism. In the early church baptism held the attention (cf. the white clothing worn for weeks, its frequent mention in liturgy, its frequent illustration in paintings and mosaics, the cult of *baptisteria*); clerical symbols developed later. The imbalance is present in the new Code of Canon Law: it regularly speaks of "sacred pastors" but never of the "sacred laity." Yet, there would be no sacred orders without sacred baptism!

The amount of attention paid to a truth should be in proportion to the importance of that truth, cf. the admonition of Vatican Council II to Catholic theologians:

When comparing doctrines, they should remember that in

... Catholic teaching there exists an order or "hierarchy" of truths, since they vary in their relationship to the foundation of the Christian faith. (UR 11)

been the subject of any final definition. The result of such conflicts may be not only a loss of respect for authority but a loosening of the bond of communion and love.[24]

*

With this, the foundations have been set and the context presented for our reflections on the teaching authority and the response of the people to its proclamations.

The good seed now is in human hands, and the spreading of it is a human operation. As always, when God's abundance meets human limitations, we struggle to understand.

[24]Some of the conflicts which developed in recent times around documents published by the Holy See may well have been caused by the method used in approaching the issues: the Holy See has not taken into account the increasingly large number of highly educated Catholics. They are willing to surrender to the truth when solemnly proclaimed, but as long as the church has not come to a final judgment, they wish to know and to weigh the arguments used in deciding an issue. This is a healthy development, a cause for rejoicing.

In circumstances when the educational level was lower, the need for explanations was less, too.

In other terms, when in affirming a point of doctrine, the teaching authority is not relying on the full assistance of the Spirit (such as in a solemn definition), but on the authority of theological reasoning; it is right and just that this reasoning should be communicated to the community so that they too may participate in the search for the whole truth.

2

TEACHING AUTHORITY

Let us return to the fundamental fact: the good seed is in the hand of the people of God; the whole church is the trustee of the word of God. In the beginning it was given to the fledgling community of the disciples who heard it, treasured and proclaimed it. The understanding of its full meaning, however, was not given to them; by God's will it was to unfold in the course of history.

In this process of unfolding, the episcopate plays a specific role. The bishops are the custodians (not exclusive possessors) of the Word. If ever divisions arise in the community concerning its essential meaning, they have the capacity to bring a judgment in the Spirit, which may not be inspired but which will not fail in truth either.

This is a sacramental task; nothing else explains it. At the final result their statement does not depend on their learning or on their holiness. By the Spirit they are prevented from giving a false testimony.

Out of such testimonies the great Creeds were born,

and in their affirmations the faithful recognized the truth of God.

While such solemn proclamations of the meaning of the Word were always rare, a quite ordinary process of understanding it at a greater depth has been going on (and is going on) all the time. In this process, too, there is a dialectical exchange between the episcopate and the whole church. As the bishops can speak with different degrees of solemnity and determination, according to the requirements of the subject matter and the historical circumstances, the response of the people must vary too.

But no matter in what way the bishops speak, they will speak in a human language with all its modulations and nuances, with all its certainties and ambiguities. If God has handed over the good seed to human persons, they will go about sowing it in their own way. No exception to that.

Magisterium

Today the common name for the teaching authority of the episcopate is magisterium. The term comes to us from the ancient Romans;[1] in subsequent ages its various meanings have been preserved in new cultural and religious contexts. It could mean either civil or ecclesiastical

[1] The *Oxford Latin Dictionary* gives the following meanings: 1. The office of superintendent, president or master. 2. Control, governance. 3. Instruction, teaching.

jurisdiction (cf. the English "magistrate") or an authority to teach (cf. the academic degree which traditionally empowered a person to teach, Magister Artium).[2] However, a restrictive and exclusive usage of it, signifying "the teaching authority of the hierarchy" began to develop among German theologians and canonists in the 18th century and became widely accepted in the 19th. Its first appearance in a papal document was probably in 1835, in an encyclical by Gregory XVI to the Swiss clergy.[3] It was used amply in the schemata of Vatican I, and from then on it became a household term in Catholic theology.

In particular, the new term, magisterium, was soon applied to a new way of exercising the teaching power: the popes began to instruct the universal church through "circular letters", that is, encyclicals. It was Gregory XVI (1831-46) who initiated the frequent use of such letters as teaching instruments; his successors followed him. Papal pronouncements on virtually everything of interest to the church kept multiplying ever since; sometimes instructing the faithful in the fundamentals of our faith, sometimes

[2]It is interesting to note that modern canon law has eliminated the venerable and ancient title of Magister from its academic hierarchy. Ignatius of Loyola, M.A. (Paris, earned), used it throughout his life; in fact, it was his preferred title. In his correspondence with Francis Xavier, M.A. (Paris, earned), who was on his apostolic journeys in India and beyond, they addressed each other by the title Magister.

[3]See Yves Congar, Droit ancien et structures ecclesiales (London: Variorum Reprints, 1982), VII: 85-98.

deciding highly technical theological issues debated among theologians. Pius IX (1846-78) published 33 encyclicals, Leo XIII (1878-1903) 48, and Pius XII (1939-58) 41— although not all of them of doctrinal interest.[4]

Behind the increasing number of encyclicals, there was a deeper change: there was a shift in the popes' own perception of their magisterium. Traditionally, they conceived their role either as called to exhort the faithful, using the common expressions of faith (the writings of Gregory the Great would be a good example of this); or, as called to decide an issue about which the church was divided (of which an example is the *Tomus I Leonis*, a clarification given by Leo the Great concerning the two natures of Christ against the heresies of Eutyches, cf. DS 296-299).

This development in the conception of the teaching office brought with it the problem of how to determine the authority of particular papal pronouncements. Since they have become so numerous and kept covering so many issues, all of them could not be of "supreme apostolic authority." Side by side with the proclamation of the evangelical message, the private opinions and personal intuitions of each pope were bound to play a much greater role than they did in earlier times when papal declarations were rare.

---

[4]*See* H. Bacht, "Enzyklika" in LTK 3:910-911. The increase in papal teaching may have been due also to the decline in vitality of the traditional schools of theology.

That was not all, however. The increased intensity of the teaching office necessitated increased help; the popes turned for assistance to individual theologians perhaps more than ever before. Not surprisingly (especially if one takes into account the difficulties in travel and communications) the popes sought help from the professors of the Roman schools of theology, and from their own curial officials who (mostly) were educated in those schools. It was only natural that the advisers tended to identify their own theological opinions with Catholic doctrine,[5] with the

---

[5]This excessive use of local theologians marked the preparatory phase of both Vatican Councils.

Vatican Council I: The Preparatory Commission was composed of five cardinals; four Italians from the curia and one Bavarian. They were helped by 96 other members and consultors, 61 of them domiciled in Rome. The first schema on Catholic faith was prepared by Johannes Franzelin, professor at the Gregorian; it was often described as a no doubt well meant attempt by a teacher to have his textbook canonized by the Council. It underwent radical revision by Joseph Kleutgen, the theologian of the Bishop of Paderborn.

Vatican Council II: Although the membership of the preparatory commissions was more international, the Roman schools of thought marked strongly the 73 documents prepared for approval, except the one on liturgy. Indeed the reform of liturgy was accepted without substantial changes; but the conflict surfaced during the debate on the second *schema* submitted to the Fathers on the "Sources of Revelation." It was mostly the work of Sebastian Tromp, reflecting his lectures at the Gregorian. For all practical purposes it was rejected, as were another 70, or (a few of them) modified so radically that the original could not be recognized. (The only one apart from Liturgy that was approved without serious modifications was the *schema* on the media of communications; it happened at a critical

result that the pronouncements of the popes began to reflect the views of Roman theologians to the exclusion of others. Examples of this can be found in the talks and writings of Pius XII, who relied very heavily on some professors from the Gregorian University. (Pius's doctrine on the Mystical Body reflected that of Sebastian Tromp; many of his moral instructions can be found in the books of Franz Hürth, etc.). Such a reliance on local advisers, who inevitably represented a limited portion of Catholic thinking, raised again the questions of how far a given papal pronouncement was the proclamation of Catholic doctrine universally held, and how far it reflected the opinion of a theological school.

In more technical terms: as a virtually new source of theological data, *locus theologicus* has emerged in recent papal pronouncements; a sound set of rules for the use of this source had to be worked out.

Historical precedents were not of much help: they carried an ambivalent message. In the course of ancient history, some solemn declarations by popes were obviously proclamations of Catholic belief, such as the condemnation of crude conciliarism (appeal from the pope to a general

moment when the Council was not in the mood to give much time or attention to it.)

The point in saying all this is that the excessive influence of Roman theologians has been resisted by the councils; but when there was no council their influence was often unhindered.

council) by Pius II (Bull *Execrabilis*, 1460); but some others promulgated with similar solemnity either had to be radically reinterpreted, such as the statement by Boniface VIII "We declare, affirm, and define that for salvation it is necessary for all human creatures to be subject to the Roman Pontiff" (Bull *Unam sanctam*, 1302); or even abandoned as totally erroneous such as the order of Innocent VIII to persecute witches, female and male, in southern Germany (Bull *Summis desiderantes*, 1484). Whatever the rules for weighing the authority of papal documents were in the past, for the age of modern encyclicals new hermeneutics were needed.

To build up such new hermeneutics was a gigantic task in itself (it is still far from being completed), and yet it was not enough. Theologians had to grapple also with instructions, decrees, declarations and many kinds of communications by the increasingly numerous and active offices and commissions of the Holy See. There, even recent history could not provide much guidance: while some documents issued by them proved to be of permanent doctrinal value, some others, such as the early decrees of the Biblical Commission, had to be quietly rescinded as mistaken in their content and method.

Besides, there was this principle to be held firmly: the charism of infallibility granted to the successors of Peter could not be delegated. It follows that the organs of the Holy See, that is the "dicasteria" of the Roman curia, could not speak "in the Spirit" as ecumenical councils could,[6] nor could they appeal to the gift of infallibility because that gift was personal to the pope and not transferable. Hence, whatever came from such offices on their own authority,[7] needed again to be evaluated according to a new set of rules—the hermeneutics applicable to the documents of the agencies of the Roman See.[8]

[6]A Roman Congregation could never say *placuit Spiritui sancto et nobis*, "it pleased the Holy Spirit and us"; an ancient formula used by great ecumenical councils.

[7]The approval by the pope of a document issued by a Roman Congregation does not necessarily indicate that the pope made the content of the document his own.

There are two kinds of papal approvals, *in common form* and *in special form*. An approval in common form means that the pope agrees to the publication of the document but does not make its content his own; an approval in special form means that the pope gives his own authority to the content of the document. The former is not papal teaching, the latter is. The special character of the approval must be explicitly stated in the document itself; it must never be presumed.

Thus to know the form of approval is crucial for the interpretation of the document; also for determining the type of response that is due to it.

[8]I do not know of any thorough study from a theological point of view of the power of the Roman curia. In general it is said that it is the arm of the pope in governing the church, which of course is true. An ambivalence that would deserve serious study is in the situation that the pope cannot hand over to anyone his charism of infallibility (fidelity to the message) but he can let others participate in his power to govern (jurisdiction).

The Curia has no more power than what the pope gives to it. An episcopal synod is different because there is an inherent power in every single bishop (through his ordination) participating in it; also because it is a partial but real manifestation of collegiality. The church discovered very

Even such a brief survey shows that the word magisterium, when used loosely, can cover several distinct
realities. Let me list them without claiming to be exhaustive:
(1) infallible teaching by the pope (rare, its core not subject
to revision); (2) non-infallible pronouncement by the pope
(can be the proclamation of truth; can be an evolving
theological opinion); (3) declaration by an office of the
Roman See, approved *specially* by the pope (he made it his
own); (4) declaration by an office, with routine approval
(by which the pope does not lend his authority to the core
of the teaching, hence its critical assessment is warranted);
(5) a great variety of pronouncements which may come
from episcopal synods, conferences, or individual bishops
(all to be weighed and measured according to their content
and circumstances).[9]

early this intrinsic value of episcopal synods; there is recorded evidence of
them from about 170. They were held quite frequently and they played an
immense role in developing the doctrine and discipline of the church; long
before a strong central government arose.

The synodal tradition is still strong in the Orthodox church. (See P.
Joannou, "Synods, Early Church" NCE 13:885-886)

[9]As a rule, in the United States there is little awareness of these subtle
distinctions among the reporters and commentators of religious events.
Whenever a document arrives from Rome, it matters little if it is a private
letter from a cardinal made public, or a decree by the authority of a
congregation, or an apostolic constitution by the authority of the pope;
they all are described as "Vatican documents," and they are attributed to
(falsely) pretty much the same authority.

To sum it up: since the exercise of the teaching office of the popes underwent a significant change, it became increasingly difficult to determine the weight of their pronouncements. (No theologian has ever succeeded in determining the specific weight of condemnation for each individual item in the *Syllabus of Errors* of Pius IX.) In particular, the enormous output of the popes, covering a very broad spectrum, made it difficult to separate what was affirmed with full apostolic authority and what represented the personal thought of a pope. Moreover, the newly established curial offices or commissions frequently took on themselves the task of deciding disputed doctrinal issues on their authority, which did not (could not) include any participation in the charism of infallibility. Quite naturally, the weight of their pronouncements became a matter of debate.

The inevitable conclusion is that, when the question arises as to how far a point of doctrine proclaimed by the magisterium is binding, the only way of finding it out is not by invoking a precise definition of the type of magisterium which appears to be operational in the case (since such definitions are hardly available) but by referring its content to our ancient traditions, by examining critically the source

At times not even the Catholic press displays a knowledge of these vital distinctions. To attribute more authority to a document than was given to it by its source is to falsify its meaning and intent, and consequently, to mislead the people.

of that pronouncement and weighing carefully the
authority behind it.

Infallible magisterium

In the common parlance and current thinking, infallibility has been connected with the papacy. Nothing
shows it better than the frequent recurrence of the
expression "papal infallibility" while hardly anyone ever
speaks about "conciliar infallibility," which is of no lesser
degree than that of the pope. The church's infallibility
which is the source of the others is mentioned only in
academic lectures.

The root of infallibility goes much deeper than the
personal wisdom of a pope or of a council, or of the whole
people of God. It is in the fidelity of the Spirit: he cannot
abandon God's chosen ones to falsehood. The Spirit who
led Jesus to preach (cf. Luke 4:1), cannot let his message go.

From the fidelity of the Spirit follows the fidelity of the
church to the evangelical message.

The episcopal college or the pope are instrumental in
this fidelity: when they solemnly proclaim the original
message, they are protected from misleading the people,
hence they cannot err, hence they are infallible—because
the faith of the church cannot be touched by corruption. If
it could, the mission which Christ has given to the apostles
could not be fulfilled.

The term "infallibility" is not the best expression to tell the whole truth. It is negative, it does not specify the object of the charism, it leaves the door open for all kinds of sinister conjectures.[10]

"Fidelity to the revelation" is a far more positive expression, and in substance it means what we intend to convey by "infallibility"; it has also a venerable history. Right from the earliest times, the Christian community believed in the unfailing fidelity of the Spirit to the church. The belief that the ecumenical councils can proclaim

---

[10]Albert Lang (University Professor at the University of Bonn) writes in *Lexikon für Theologie und Kirche*:

> The term "infallibility", in use since the late scholastic times, and dominant since the Council of Trent, was an infelicitous choice (*nicht glücklich gewahlt*); in its unrestricted generality it is arrogant (*anmassend*) and overbearing (*überheblich*), especially when in a one-sided fashion it brings the infallibility of the pope into the foreground. It leads easily to the misconception that the charism of infallibility excludes other types of failures in the exercise of the teaching office, such as imprudence, human weaknesses, moral failure, inaction and similar ones. Moreover, it generates a fear that the pope on the ground of his infallibility could claim an unrestricted jurisdiction to govern and to judge. But these are caricatures and distorted presentations of infallibility. (LTK 10:485)

If the use of a word can give occasion for such distortions, it is reasonable to ask if the same reality could not be described better by another word; especially if we wish to facilitate the ecumenical dialogue and make easier for unbelivers the understanding of the Christian doctrine.

unfailingly "what is contained in the Scriptures" or what is an integral part of God's revelation, developed precisely from this steady conviction.[11] One could wish Vatican Council I had chosen a better expression! Be that as it may, Vatican Council I defined infallibility in a very cautious and circumscribed way. It is safe to say that a large portion of the hierarchical teaching, as it is exercised now, does not fall into that category. Therefore the precise understanding of what is meant by non-infallible teaching is more important than ever.[12]

[11]After all, one could ask if there is any Christian church or ecclesial community which does not believe in this unfailing fidelity of the Spirit to the "gathering" of Christians. Each group may see the ultimate mani-festation of this fidelity in different ways: in the definitions of an ecumenical council, or in the reading of the Scriptures coupled with an internal enlightenment in the reader, or in a convocation of clergy and laity, etc. If a Christian group did not believe in this fidelity of the Spirit to them, they could never be sure that they still have the authentic message of Christ.

Catholics differ from the others not so much in their belief in infallibility (all communities seem to have that) but in seeing the instruments or agents or the criteria of infallibility in a different way from the others.

[12]A theologian conscious of history will be always careful not to draw the dividing line too sharply between the infallibly defined and the not-so-defined beliefs. After all, for many centuries there was no such distinction; there was a unity of beliefs. Gradually, through councils and papal statements some parts of the beliefs have been specially marked as containing no error; some other parts have not been so marked, but for that they have not lost their organic connection with the rest.

Non-infallible magisterium

The "non-infallible" teaching is really composed of two organically united strata of doctrine: it contains part of God's revelation and (mixed or fused with it) it includes changeable human thoughts. Simple statements, such as "non-infallible proclamations are not binding"; or "non-infallible statements by ecclesiastical authorities are binding" do not pay enough attention or respect to the complex character of the body of "non-infallible" beliefs.

Indeed, no one has ever asserted that all that we have to believe has been the object of infallible pronouncements. It follows that we must handle the beliefs that have not been infallibly defined cautiously; some of it (perhaps a great deal of it) may be part of God's revelation. When a point of doctrine was peacefully believed and no crisis developed around it, no council or pope ever thought of infallibly defining it.

An infallible "determination" (ancient councils preferred that term to "definition") means that a point of belief has been marked, specially authenticated; but there are other points which have not been so singled out yet are no less true than those so "determined."

Once this much is admitted (how could it be denied?), it becomes obvious that there is an organic unity between "determined" and "not-determined" truth; between doctrine infallibly proclaimed and doctrine non-infallibly taught.

To separate within the "non-infallible" portion of beliefs the incorrect expressions of our faith from what are human opinions is not easy. To determine if a given point of doctrine is an integral part of revelation or not, it is necessary to examine the precise content of that doctrine, its place in Christian tradition, its connection with other mysteries. Such inquiry is always a slow process, and can be full of pitfalls. It requires a good deal of historical knowledge and training in methodology. Indeed, theological research has become a no less sophisticated activity than research in (e.g.) theoretical physics—with the additional limitation that no verification can be done by experiments.[13]

[13]It is interesting to compare the style of publications in theoretical physics, with publications in systematic theology. At times, the difference is striking. The physicists, after their expositions and explanations, tend to stress how much more they do not know and consequently they display a reluctance to make final and apodictic statements. The theologians after they have given their presentations and clarifications tend to come to firm and decisive statements concerning the ultimate truth of the matter. Is this because the scientists know that nature is there and quite ready to correct them, while the theologians know that a correction out of a supernatural world is not likely?

I submit that this tendency among theologians (of diffferent denominations?) is a survival of the post-Tridentine method (remember the controversalists?), which postulated that every inquiry should begin with a thesis to be defended, not with a question to be investigated—as was customary in the middle ages, cf. the *sic-et-non* method of Abelard and the *Quaestiones* in the works of Aquinas.

One wonders if the "thesis method" already current in the sixteenth century has contributed to the bitter tone of the Reformation controversies and made reconciliation more difficult.

What is ordinary magisterium?

Non-infallible magisterium is referred to also as ordinary magisterium. Immediately, a cautionary word should be sounded about what is "ordinary." The term has undergone a significant transformation in the last two or so decades, particularly noticeable in the official language of the Holy See, be it in writings, be it in oral statements.

The expression "ordinary magisterium" in the standard theology textbooks published before Vatican Council II used to refer to the manner (*modus*) in which a point of doctrine was determined as an integral part of our faith: not through the rather extraordinary act of a decree by a council, not through the extraordinary event of a papal definition, but through its consistent affirmation *as Catholic doctrine* by the popes and the bishops (in Vatican II terminology, by the college of bishops). For all practical purposes such an ordinary teaching was equivalent to a formal definition.

Interestingly enough this understanding of "ordinary magisterium" is retained in the new Code of Canon Law:

> All that is contained in the word of God, as has been handed over in writing or by tradition, that is, [*all*] that is in the one deposit of faith entrusted to the church, and is proclaimed either by the solemn magisterium of the church, or by its ordinary and universal magisterium, which becomes manifest in the common assent

of the faithful under the guidance of the sacred magisterium, must be believed with divine and Catholic faith; . . . all are bound, therefore, to reject doctrines contrary to it. (Canon 750)[14]

The canon clearly implies that there are two ways of teaching infallibly: by solemn magisterium or by ordinary magisterium. But the expression "ordinary magisterium" is used also in a different way, in particular by Roman authorities:

> . . . the Church does not build its life upon its infallible magisterium alone but on the teaching of its authentic, ordinary magisterium as well. (*Sacra Congregatio pro Doctrina Fidei*, July 25, 1986, *Re Curran*.)[15]

[14]The text of the canon is taken from the Constitution *Dei Filius* by Vatican Council I; cf. DS 3011.

On the basis of this text, the suggestion could be made that ordinary *and* universal teaching is infallible, while ordinary and non-universal is fallible. But the term *universal* is not precise enough to ground such an important distinction. After all, the ministry of Peter's successor is certainly universal, his proclamations are, as a rule, addressed to the whole church, hence have a universal character, but without having necessarily the character of infallibility. The same could be said of the college of bishops: Vatican Council II was certainly a universal gathering; its proclamations could not have been more universal; yet, no one has ever asserted that they are infallible in all their parts.

[15]*See* Charles E. Curran, *Faithful Dissent*, (Kansas City: Sheed & Ward, 1986), p. 268. Cf. also Page, *Qui est l'Eglise?*, vol. 3, p. 547: he warns about the different senses of *magistere ordinaire*.

The statement is substantially correct, but undoubtedly it uses the expression "ordinary magisterium" in a sense different from the one in the canon quoted; "ordinary" now is opposed to "infallible". It refers to something less than the proclamation of a point of belief with full and final apostolic authority (whether in council or otherwise); it means simply the ordinary and usual teaching and preaching activity of the hierarchy, affirming a point of doctrine which (as yet) cannot be said to be part of our Catholic faith because (as yet) the church has not affirmed it with a conclusive judgment.

To call such teaching "ordinary magisterium" is a relatively new use of the term "ordinary." In theory such an ambivalence in its meaning should cause no serious problem, provided we are aware of it, but in practice conflicts are bound to break out when ecclesiastical authorities begin to demand the same absolute obedience to their usual teaching and preaching as is due only to articles of faith, or when they attempt to impose their views with heavy (or subtle) penalties on all those who see the matter otherwise.[16]

[16]In the years after Vatican Council II there has been much talk about "creeping infallibility," meaning the tendency to regard doctrines not infallibly defined as if they had been so defined. To hold such exaggerations on a purely intellectual level is already bad enough, but when practical sanctions are taken against someone who does not accept them, the situation becomes even worse. Failure in truth may lead to failure in justice . . . (One more reason to promote sound, loyal and critical theological reflection!)

Is there a magisterium of doctors?

Some years ago Avery Dulles suggested another refinement in the understanding of magisterium: he proposed that we should speak of a dual magisterium, one exercised by the hierarchy, another by the theologians.[17] Although Dulles could invoke good medieval authorities (among them Gratian and Aquinas) to support his view, Francis Sullivan in his book *Magisterium* is opposed to such a use mainly from a pastoral point of view.[18] I am inclined to agree with Sullivan, given the evolution of the concept of magisterium and its meaning *today*. To speak of two magisteria could lead to endless confusion.

But an opinion about the use of a term does not necessarily decide the merits of an issue. Indeed, side by side with the hierarchical magisterium, there has been continually another kind of magisterium in the church. Moreover, the church has not failed in according solemn

[17]See CTSA *Proceedings* 35 (1980), pp. 155-169.

[18]"In my view, it would cause confusion and lead to misunderstanding, to use the term *magisterium* nowadays to describe the role of theologians and exegetes, and so to insist on there being a twofold *magisterium* in the church. The fact is that in modern usage, the term *magisterium* has come to be associated exclusively with pastoral teaching authority." See Sullivan, *Magisterium*, p. 29.

recognition (rarely adverted to) to this non-hierarchical teaching power.[19]

Let me explain. As we have seen in the first section of this essay, the deposit of revelation has been handed over to the whole church; it is in the possession of the whole body, not in the exclusive possession of the hierarchy. Peter was called the rock on which the church was to be built; he was never called the "church", nor were the twelve. (The modern usage of saying that "the church" has spoken or has done this-and-that when in fact an office or an official has spoken or acted, is theologically incorrect and misleading; a better usage would be to name the office or the official involved, such as "The Congregation of the Doctrine of the Faith stated," or, "The bishop of . . . ordered," etc.)

Vatican Council I is quite explicit in affirming that the revelation has been received by, and belongs to the whole church when it says that the pope has that infallibility with which the church is endowed.

> The Roman Pontiff when he speaks *ex cathedra* . . . has [*pollere*] `that infallibility with which the divine Redeemer wanted his church to be endowed in defining doctrine concerning faith and morals. (DS 3074)

---

[19]Those Catholics who strongly deny that there is a non-hierarchical teaching charism in the church, should oppose also, if they wish to be logical, the calling of anyone who was not ordained bishop "doctor of the church."

If any doubt remains it should be dispelled by the plain speech of Vatican Council II:

> The body of the faithful as a whole, anointed as they are by the Holy One (cf. Jn. 2:20, 27), cannot err in matters of belief. Thanks to a supernatural sense of faith which characterizes the People as a whole, it manifests its unerring quality when, 'from the bishops down to the last member of the laity' (Cf. St. Augustine, *De praed. sanct.* 14, 27), it shows universal agreement in matters of faith and morals." (LG 12)

Once it is clear and accepted that revelation is in the possession of the whole church, it becomes obvious that all believers have access to it; all can perceive it, witness its truth, have insights into its depths.

It is at this point that the difference between the specific task and charism of the hierarchy and of the theologians (some ancient sources prefer to use the expression "the interpreters of the Scriptures") can be distinguished.

The specific vocation of the popes and bishops is to be witnesses to the truth of evangelical doctrine ("you shall be my witnesses . . . to the end of the earth," cf. Act 1:8), which does not necesarily include the capacity to have the deepest insight into the content of the mysteries. I am not suggesting that popes and bishops could not have such a gift; many did, Ambrose, Augustine, Anselm are outstanding examples. But new insights into the mysteries require other qualifications than ordination.

Indeed, there have been other persons in the church (whether we should call them interpreters of the Scriptures or theologians is immaterial), who were not in any hierarchical position yet had an extraordinary capacity to penetrate the mysteries to an unusual depth and the gift to articulate their discoveries for the whole community. The most resounding recognition on the part of the church has come to them always posthumously when they were declared doctors of the church. In such a declaration the church is not adding anything to their heavenly status; it merely recognizes what they have been in their earthly life: teachers and "magisters" for the whole church.

Obviously, I do not mean that all those who had the title of, say, theologian had also the gift of genuine insights; there were many "prophets" in Israel who did not speak the word of God. Yet, the fact stands that while the hierarchy, popes and bishops kept the faith intact in all ages, some of the most significant developments came from persons who were not in the episcopal order.

Thomas Aquinas has been named the *doctor communis*, the common teacher of the whole church, conceivably for all ages. Teresa of Avila has been honored as *doctor vitae spiritualis*. John Henry Newman has been an inspiration for more recent developments in theology, including the teaching of Vatican Council II, and he may well be recognized one day as the *doctor subtilis* of the nineteenth century.

Moreover, the immense influence exercised at Vatican Council II by the experts who were not bishops is well known.

So, there has always been a genuine and recognized magisterium by others than popes and bishops: the magisterium of graced, learned and wise men and women to whom it was given to have new insights into the old truths.

Magister Gratianus (around 1140) has a small piece on this issue, which is a jewel in its brevity. I am not sure what is more significant, the fact that he wrote it, or the fact that no one took offense; not even the Roman correctors when they "revised" the *Decretum* after the Council of Trent. The Master was defining the various degrees of authority in the church; after he stated that the decretal letters of the popes have the same rank as the canons of the councils, he raised the question about the authority of the *expositores scripturarum*, the interpreters of the sacred Scriptures.

> Now the question is about the interpreters of the sacred Scriptures; are their writings of the same rank [as the decretal letters] or are they subject to them? The more someone is grounded in reason, the greater authority his words seem to have. Many of the interpreters, being more eminent than others in the grace of the holy Spirit and in ample learning, can be shown also to be better grounded in reason. Therefore, it seems, preference should be given to the sayings of Augustine, Jerome and other writers over the consti-

tutions of some pontiffs. But there is a difference between deciding cases [*causas*] and diligently interpreting the scriptures. To decide cases learning is not enough, power, too, is needed . . . it appears [therefore] that those who interpret the divine scriptures, although they are more eminent in learning than the pontiffs, in deciding cases [*causas*] must take their places after the pontiffs, because they have not been raised to the same pontifical dignity; in the exposition of the Scriptures, however, they must be placed before the pontiffs.[20]

[20]This is a sensitive passage; it deserves to be quoted fully in the original:

Decretales itaque epistolae canonibus conciliorum pari iure exequantur. Nunc autem queritur de expositoribus sacrae scripturae, an exequentur, an subiciantur eis? Quo enim quisque magis ratione nititur, eo maioris auctoritatis eius verba esse videntur. Plurimi autem tractatorum, sicut pleniori gratia Spiritus sancti, ita ampliori scientia aliis precellentes, rationi magis adhesisse probantur. Unde nonnullorum Pontificum constitutis Augustini, Ieronimi atque aliorum tractatorum dicta eis videntur esse preferenda.

Sed aliud est causis terminum imponere aliud scripturas sacras diligenter exponere. Negotiis diffiniendis non solum est necessaria scientia, sed etiam potestas. Unde Christus dicturus Petro: "Quodcumque ligaveris super terram, erit ligatum et in coelis, etc." prius dedit sibi claves regni coelorum: in altera dans ei scientiam discernendi inter lepram et lepram, in altera sibi potestatem eiciendi aliquos ab ecclesia, vel recipiendi. Cum ergo quaelibet negotia finem accipiant vel in absolutione innocentium, vel in condempnatione delinquentium, absolutio vero vel condempnatio non scientiam tantum, sed etiam potestatem presidentium desiderant: apparet, quod divinarum scripturarum

The text itself needs some interpretation; but undeniably Gratian was aware of a teaching authority in the church that has its source not in the episcopal ordination but in the grace of the holy Spirit, the knowledge of the Scriptures and sound reasoning. He goes so far as to say that at times such an authority can prevail over a pontifical document. Arguably, one must not simply substitute "theologians" (as we understand it today) for the "interpreters of scriptures"; Gratian may have been thinking principally of the Fathers of the church.

Further, Gratian clearly conceived a final doctrinal pronouncement by those who had pontifical (episcopal) authority as a judicial act; it terminated a "case." For him the bishops were the final judges in doctrinal disputes which arose among the faithful.

Indeed, the pope and his brother bishops can be correctly described as the final judges of what belongs to the doctrine of faith, as *iudices fidei*; yet the very same expression is unsatisfactory under other aspects. A judicial act is a jurisdictional act; to proclaim the evangelical

tractatores, etsi scientia Pontificibus premineant, tamen, quia dignitatis eorum apicem non sunt adepti, in sacrarum scripturarum expositionibus eis preponuntur, in causis vero diffiniendis secundum post eos locum merentur.

There is a clear distinction, if there ever was one, between the power of jurisdiction and the power of interpreting the Scriptures! (See *Dictum* before canon I, Distinctio XX in *Decretum Magistri Gratiani*, ed. Aemilius Friedberg [Graz: Akademische Verlagsanstalt, 1959] col. 65.)

message is much more than that. Also, in the Scriptures the principal task given to the apostles is to be witnesses of the great events of our redemption. To restrict the episcopal teaching to judicial decisions only would not do justice to the charism of their office.

For these reasons, throughout this book I prefer to use scriptural expression and describe the task of the bishops as that of being the authentic witnesses of the great events of our redemption.

Obviously, I do not mean to deny (I rather steadily affirm) that every Christian has to be a witness of the same events. The bishops, however, are qualified witnesses: through their ordination they have been designated as principal preachers, and when the community is divided, their testimony about the truth is the final and authentic one—through the invisible and gracious assistance of the Spirit.

But the issue of the authority of the bishops as compared to that of the theologians was clearly a disputed question in the medieval schools; Aquinas returned to it a century later. He distinguished two cathedras: magisterial and pontifical. Here is his most elaborate text on the topic:

> . . . there is a threefold difference between the magisterial cathedra and the pontifical cathedra.
>
> The first is that he who receives a magisterial cathedra, does not receive any eminence that he has not had before; he receives only an opportunity, which

he did not have before, to communicate his science...
But he who receives an episcopal cathedra, receives an
eminence of power, which he did not have before; as
regards power, he was like all the others.

The second difference is that the eminence of
science, which is required for the magisterial cathedra,
is a perfection residing in the person; the eminence of
power is attributed to a person only in relation to
others.

The third difference is that a person becomes apt for
a pontifical cathedra by being outstanding in charity;
but for a magisterial cathedra a person becomes apt
through having sufficient learning.[21]

[21]In the original Latin:

...oportet triplicem differentiam considerare cathedrae magistralis ad cathedram pontificalem.

Quarum prima est, quod ille qui accipit cathedram magistralem, non accipit aliquam eminentiam quam prius non
habuerit, sed solum opportunitatem communicandi scientiam,
quam prius non habebat: ...Ille vero qui accipit cathedram
episcopalem, accipit eminentiam potestatis, quam prius non
habebat, sed quantum ad hoc in nullo ab aliis differebat.

Secunda differentia est, quod eminentia scientiae, quae
requiritur ad cathedram magistralem, est perfectio hominis
secundum se ipsum; eminentia vero potestatis, quae pertinet ad
cathedram pontificalem, est hominis per comparationem ad
alium.

Tertia differentia est, quod ad cathedram pontificalem fit
homo idoneus per caritatem excellentem; ...ad cathedram
autem magistralem redditur homo idoneus ex sufficientia
scientiae. (*Quodl.* 3, 9, c)

Aquinas's mind was certainly not that in the church there were two independent *magisteria* of equal standing; he saw the two cathedras as operating on different levels and as performing different tasks. From the one, learning was communicated to the community, from the other decisions were made, including final decisions when the community was divided on a doctrinal issue of some substance; which meant that when an article of faith was contested the *cathedra magistralis* was subject to the *cathedra pontificalis.*[22]

[22]The passage about the two cathedras quoted above appears in an "article" entitled *Is it permissible for someone to request for himself the licence to teach theology?* (There is the issue of the "canonical mission" as it was played out in the thirteenth century!) Thomas's answer is *"yes"*:

> Since the one who receives licence to occupy a magisterial cathedra receives only the opportunity to communicate what he has, to ask for such a licence in itself contains no wrong [*nullam turpitudinem continere*]; because to communicate to others the learning one has is praiseworthy and belongs to charity . . . But this rule does not apply in the same way to those who seek the licence to teach and those who seek a pontifical office [*episcopate*]. The reason is that someone can know with certainty that he has the learning that qualifies him for teaching; but no one can know with certainty that he has the charity that would qualify him for pastoral office. Therefore, it is always wrong [*vitiosum*] to ask for the pontifical office . . .

Paul appears as having been of a different opinion:

> The saying is sure: If any one aspires to the office of bishop, he desires a noble task. (1 Tim. 3:1)

If holy and learned theologians could have had a special authority in the earlier centuries, there is no reason to deny that similarly blessed persons can have it today. Magisterium may not be the best term today to describe their ministry; yet, under whatever name, we need their specific service. Nor should this service be conceived as separated from, or opposed to, that of the hierarchy; ultimately whatever insight they may have into the mysteries, if it is authentic, cannot be different from what the popes and bishops are witnessing.

The organic unity of Christian doctrine

Yes, there is an organic unity of Christian doctrine. All that has been infallibly determined or defined belongs to it. A great deal of what has not been so singled out belongs to it. But there is much among the non-infallible teaching that is human opinion.

As we have seen earlier, the division of our beliefs into two neat categories, infallible and fallible, coupled with the suggestion that dissent from non-infallibly stated doctrine should be always permissible, is a simplistic approach to a complex issue.[23] Some of the non-infallibly stated doctrines

---

[23]Besides it displays a lack of sensitivity for history. Should one conclude that before the Council of Nicaea (325), where the first major definitions occurred, Christians could dissent from any part of the tradition handed down to them?

may well be integral parts of divine revelation.

It follows also, with no less force, that many non-infallible propositions are no more than respectable school opinions, and as such, they are not part of the universally held Catholic doctrine. Theologians should not be easily castigated for criticizing or rejecting such teachings; to say that *all* non-infallible statements form an organic unity with infallible doctrine is nonsense.

A particularly difficult issue in determining the boundaries of the Catholic doctrine in its organic unity is in the field of morality. There is no doubt that the evangelical message includes particular moral precepts: it tells us about God's mighty deeds and *the way* to the Father. The church cannot be less competent in proclaiming this way than it is competent in narrating the story of our redemption.

But there is no evidence that answers to *all* issues of morality that human beings can ever face are somehow given in Christian revelation, or can be deduced from it, or somehow can develop from it. There are complex problems in bioethics, in economy, in politics for which Christian tradition offers no clear guidance. At most, the church could invoke a philosophical system and solve a problem with the help of some principles derived from it, as for instance Pius XII has invoked the "principle of totality" to decide how far the transplant of an organ from one living person to another could be allowed—or should be forbidden.[24] The result may be an honest and prudent attempt to find a solution; but it is doubtful that the position taken can be part of the organic unity of Christian doctrine. After all, the church always refused to canonize any philosophical system; hence an affirmation grounded in philosophy must not be easily admitted into the realm of the "evangelical message."[25]

There is nothing in our tradition that would forbid the view that there are moral issues concerning the temporal and secular order which must be solved with the help of

[24]*See* "Mutilation" in NCE 10: 145-146, and "Organic Transplants," *ibid.* 754-756; also (and especially) the article by Gerald Kelly "Pope Pius XII and the Principle of Totality" in *Theological Studies*, 16 (1955), pp. 373-396.

[25]Vatican Council I, in defining papal infallibility, said that the pope has that infallibility "with which the divine Redeemer wanted his church to be endowed in defining the doctrine concerning faith and morals" (cf. DS 3074). The Council did not go into the description of the precise limits of this gift—as usual, the Fathers left it to the theologians to work on the problem. Questions remain: What are the limits of this infallibility? What is the meaning of "doctrine of morals"? Does it include moral precepts which in no way can be found in the revelation? Is the church the proclaimer and guardian of "natural law"? How can the church know the natural law if it is not contained in the revelation? There is always a problem with building an argument from natural law and then calling the conclusion part of Catholic teaching. On the one hand, the ecumenical councils have steadily refused to commit the church to a philosophical system, no matter how suitable or helpful it appeared; on the other hand, no statement about natural law is possible without invoking a philosophical system.

human intelligence and ingenuity, without any specific guidance from revelation. If that is the case, it follows that the church should help and respect any honest attempt to solve them, but it should claim no divine authority to impose a solution.

In other terms, the limits of the organic unity of Christian doctrine in the field of morality are not, as yet, clearly determined.

Excursus: prudential decisions by popes and bishops

What follows can be called an excursus, yet the matter we touch on is organically connected with the issue of the magisterium. We have seen how the Spirit protects the college of bishops or the pope speaking in the name of the whole college; through his providence, he prevents them from error when they solemnly authenticate a point of doctrine.

But what about practical decisions by popes and bishops? How far are they guided and protected by the Spirit in matters prudential?

Before answering those questions, let us make one point

See the judicious treatment of this issue in Sullivan, *Magisterium*, pp. 138-152. His position is that while there are good reasons to hold that particular norms of natural law are not objects of infallible teaching; they can be objects of magisterial teaching.

It follows (my remark) that we need a distinct type of hermeneutics for magisterial documents which deal with the natural law.

clear: no amount of human imprudence or neglect on the part of anyone can ever destroy the fundamental orientation and the actual progress of the church toward the fullness of the Kingdom of God; that much the Spirit guarantees. The good news will be announced to the end of time.

Once this is clear, we can return to our initial questions. The answer is that the pope and the episcopal college have been granted the charism of infallibility in matters of doctrine, but they have not been guaranteed the highest degree of prudence in matters of practical policy. There is nothing new in this statement for those who are familiar with the history of the church.

There is a difference between seeing the truth, and reaching out for a value. Truth is one and indivisible, either we surrender to it or not. Prudence has degrees, and history proves amply what theology knows in theory: popes and bishops can fail in reaching its highest degree; in fact they can fail to act prudently altogether.

This statement, however, needs immediate qualifications. It is not to say that the Spirit cannot guide those in the episcopal order in practical matters; he certainly can and he certainly does. But there is no guarantee of indefectibility in matters of prudence. Not even when a great solemnity surrounds the decision, as happened (to quote an example) when Pope Urban II launched the first crusade at Clermont in 1095. It follows that the practical decisions and actions of the popes and bishops are legitimate subject-matter for evaluation. In fact, such evaluations have been done on an immense scale by historians; all one has to do is to read Pastor's well known *History of the Popes*, highly praised by many popes.

Often, there is an illegitimate transfer, perhaps inadvertently. The rules concerning *obsequium* in the case of teaching are transferred to practical decisions, and the same intellectual respect or submission is required and given to a practical decision which is due to doctrinal proclamations only.

From all this, an important consequence follows: in merely practical matters, the episcopate ought to be advised, protected and controlled not only because of human frailty, but also for theological reasons; prudence in practical decisions and actions is not guaranteed by the Spirit. The official documents of the church may not stress this doctrine, but canon law is certainly mindful of it. For instance, in every diocese there must be a financial committee (see canons 492 - 494) which has far-ranging powers to prevent the bishop from making mistakes, including the right to stop him from making unsound transactions.

*

With this, our reflections on the teaching authority (including a short note on the practical decision-making authority) are now concluded. Let us turn our attention to the response of the people.

3

ASSENT AND DISSENT

We know that the whole church is the trustee of the word of God; we know also that the episcopate plays a special role in the preserving and unfolding of the Word in the course of history.

We know also that there is a sacred dialectic going on all the time between the episcopate and the people. In the previous section we have reflected on the pronouncements of those who have authority in matters doctrinal; in this section the scope of our reflections will be the response of the people. Let us remember, though, that *people* here may well include everyone; popes and bishops of modern times are part of the whole church which responds to the great councils of the early times.

The response, of course, must correspond to the call. If the episcopate brought solemn witness to the Word, the response cannot be anything else than a surrender in faith; if the episcopate speaks with authority but still searching for the whole truth promised by their Lord, the response of the community ought to be an *obsequium* which, depending on the certainty the church has reached, can be anything from an assent of faith to a respectful pondering how further progress toward the whole truth can be made.

When surrender in faith is due

Within the great community of the church, there is the community of the bishops. Ever since the beginnings, there has been a belief in the consciousness of the Christians that they, the bishops, when in communion with each other, have a power "in the Spirit" to proclaim the authentic word of God. Vatican Council II did no more than to articulate this ancient belief:

> Although the individual bishops do not enjoy the prerogative of infallibility, they can nevertheless proclaim Christ's doctrine infallibly. This is so, even when they are dispersed around the world, provided that while maintaining the bond of unity among themselves and with Peter's successor, and while teaching authentically on a matter of faith or morals, they concur in a single viewpoint as the one which must be held conclusively. This authority is even more clearly verified when, gathered together in an ecumenical council, they are teachers and judges of faith and morals for the universal Church; their definitions

must then be adhered to with the submission of faith.
(LG 25)

"With the submission of faith" translates *fidei obsequio*,
which means: surrender to the truth with an act of faith.
Indeed there is the sacred play: the bishops in
communion assisted by the Spirit bear witness to the truth;
the people of God, guided by the same Spirit, recognize the
truth in their voice; as they accept it they surrender their
mind to God. An act of worship: *obsequium fidei*.

The image of a sacred play is not merely an abstract
construct. The play is enacted every time a Christian
community recites the traditional (Nicene-Constantino-
politan) Creed. When they do so, usually before the
celebration of the Eucharist, they respond to the ancient
councils. There is a timeless beauty in this ceremony: far
away in space and in time, at Nicaea in 325 and in
Constantinople in 381, the assembled bishops proclaimed
the Word through a Creed they composed. Today
Christian communities respond by accepting their witness
and surrendering with an act of faith to the truth of what
they heard, notwithstanding the immense distances in
space and time.

No more need be said here about this assent in faith; the
Dogmatic Constitution on the Church, *Lumen gentium*
explicates the doctrine in some detail concerning the
particular charisms of the pope, of the episcopal college and
of the faithful.

The meaning of obsequium

The small word *obsequium* is occupying an increasingly large place in the attention of theologians.[1] No wonder: it has become a key word to describe (or to prescribe) the response of the faithful to the pronouncements of the teaching authority. To find its meaning in the original Latin is difficult enough, to translate this meaning into English is near impossible.

It may look like an abstract term, but it is meant to be practical. It has been used, and is being used, to regulate the attitude of the faithful in doctrinal matters.

In order to explain the meaning of *obsequium*, a small diversion about the hermeneutics of conciliar texts is necessary.

Often enough, there is a conciliar text in which a term or an expression is used which, at the time of the council did not have a fully matured and commonly agreed on definition; such as *subsistit* in the sentence *Haec Ecclesia [Christi]* . . . *subsistit in Ecclesia catholica* . . . "This Church [of Christ] . . . subsists in the Catholic Church. . . (LG 8). Or, *communitas ecclesialis* for describing some non-Catholic Christian communities (e.g. UR 19). Or even

[1] In the documents of Vatican Council II the word or its derivatives occur repeatedly (Ochoa in his *Index* lists twenty-two references), but it is used in a variety of senses. In the Code of Canon Law, 1983, it occurs five times, three times specifically connected with the teaching office (canons 218, 752, 753).

such a locution as *Vicarius Christi* used for both the pope
and the diocesan bishop (e.g. LG 18 and 27). Many other
examples could be quoted. The fact stands that not rarely,
when the council made a statement, especially a statement
containing a new insight into the doctrine revealed by
God, the Fathers left also some uncertainty or ambiguity
behind. No one who is familiar with the documents can
deny that much. Had it been otherwise (that is, had the
council come out with clear and distinct statements only),
its speech would not have been human speech.[2]

[2]A conventional method to explain the "mind of the council" is from
the discussions which have taken place in the drafting committees, from
the developments of the successive drafts of a document and from the
official *Relatio* which introduced it to the assembly. Such a historical
approach (indispensable as it is) can certainly account, perhaps to a high
degree, for the "mind of the committee," or the "mind of the relator," but
in itself it is incomplete because it does not account for what went on in the
mind of the vast majority who ultimately approved of the document. It is
precisely in this general act of approval that the *sensus fidei* of the episcopate
could have been playing a decisive role beyond and above the reasoning of
the drafting committee and the persuasive speech of the relator.

It follows that *a seminal concept can contain more than what the drafting
committee intended to put there.* This should not be surprising; for a long time
we have accepted that an expression in the Scriptures can contain an
inspiration for the whole church well beyond the meaning intended by the
writer himself.

All seminal locutions emerge with a meaning from the past, but their
full significance can unfold in the future only. The historians of the council
can report on the reasons articulated by the drafting committee explaining
the use of a term such as *subsistit, collegium, vicarius,* or *obsequium,* etc.; they
can have, however, no direct access to the instinct of faith of the majority
who recognized in the expression a genuine insight into the Christian

As soon as the council had come to an end, researchers converged on its pronouncements. Naturally enough, they perceived the uncertainties and ambiguities. The question came spontaneously: What did the council mean *exactly* when it used such-and-such a term or expression? Many researchers rushed (and are still rushing) into answering the question without ever asking if the Fathers intended an exact meaning in the first place as the conclusion of their thought process, or wanted to prompt the church into a thought process with the help of an intuitive insight.[3]

tradition—to be reflected on and defined with greater precision by generations to come.

In other words, the final formulation is due not only to the rational planning of a committee but also the faith vision of all the participants.

[3] I do not know of any comprehensive study (if such a thing is possible) of the hermeneutics of the declarations of Vatican Council II. There are particular studies on individual documents but they lack the dimension which can come only from comparing one document to another. If such a major study will ever be undertaken, it should include also an identification and critical evaluation of the different literary forms used within various constitutions, decrees and declarations.

Such a study is all the more needed in that Vatican Council II has been different from all other councils; its scope was not to determine contested issues but to give pastoral guidance to the whole church. Judges speak in a court room, their language is precise and technical, they absolve the innocent and condemn the guilty . Pastors speak in a friendly environment, they use words to attract and encourage those who listen, they wish to heal the sick and bring back the lost ones.

Obviously it would be wrong to say that an ecumenical council is either judicial or pastoral; nevertheless there can be dominant trends at a council

Thus dissertations and hypotheses keep multiplying, defending one meaning or another, presuming always that *there must have been* a well-defined meaning somewhere. It can be only a matter of patience and diligence to find it! Alas, at times, a monumental work "proving" what the council meant *exactly* can be described only with the classical words: *magnus passus extra viam*, a remarkable step—in the wrong direction.[4]

The thesis (if a thesis it is) I wish to put forward is that in the conciliar documents there are terms and expressions for which we need a new category. They are not precise concepts; they are "seminal locutions." This, of course, needs explanation.

Seminal locution is an expression which conveys an insight into the truth but without defining it with precision; it needs to be developed further. It is a broad and

which must be taken into account in construing the correct hermeneutics for the interpretation of that council.

[4]The emphasis is on *what the council meant exactly.* Clearly, it is perfectly legitimate to write a dissertation on the development of a point of doctrine in the discussions of a conciliar committee, or on the doctrine expounded and embraced by a relator, and so forth; as long as the researcher states conclusions with the mind of the council.

To say that the council has left room for further development in the understanding of a concept is not to imply that the council acted on scarce information about its meaning. Quite the contrary; the Fathers perceived with great clarity a meaning which carried in itself the potential for further development.

intuitive approach to a mystery that leaves plenty of room for future discoveries.[5]

For some scholars this can sound like an absurd statement; it seems to imply that the Fathers did not even know with any certainty what they were doing or saying. Well, the problem is not with the Fathers; they knew well enough what they were doing. It is with the expectation of the researchers: they assume that the council had to speak with clear and distinct ideas all the time. But this was not the case. Vatican Council II was a pastoral council not only in what it said but in the manner of saying it. In this respect, it has no parallel in history.

Besides, the same council affirmed the existence of a "supernatural sense of faith" of an "unerring quality" "from the bishops down ... which is aroused and sustained by the Spirit of truth" (LG 12). This sense of faith, no doubt, operated at the council itself, among the bishops, and helped them to identify, but not to dissect, analyze and classify, the seeds of truth which in due course can grow into a large tree.[6]

---

[5]Such a development is not simply a logical explicitation of what is contained in the seminal locution. It arises out of the convergence and accumulation of new insights, reached through reflections (and through experiences, if such is the case) prompted by the original seminal locution.

[6]Indeed, research into the meaning of a conciliar idea can go in the wrong direction, and end up with irrelevant conclusions, because of the false initial assumption that the council's intention was to teach through precise concepts and conclusive propositions. The council's task was to

All those who in one way or another were involved in the work of the council or had the opportunity to observe its operation, know well that while the Fathers had an overall perception as to "where the council was going," many of them would have been hard put to define the precise meaning of an idea they otherwise approved of and voted for. Further, if somebody had asked each individual bishop to give, before he voted, his own interpretation of, say, *subsistit*, there would have been a variety of responses - their name would have been legion! From so many differing perceptions, no ultimate precision could arise. But the multiplicity of answers could still cover a common insight and point in the same direction.

So, often enough, the right questions in undertaking the interpretation of a conciliar term and expression are: "How can this insight be developed further?" "Where does it lead?" In answering such questions Newman's theory on the development of doctrine can be helpful: enlightenment will not come from logical deductions alone; the "supernatural sense of faith" of the community will play a capital

bear witness to the truth; such a task is often correctly fulfilled by pointing toward the truth.

This is not to mean that the Fathers never used words and terms in an exact way, or they never taught in precise propositions. They did, and when they did, the meaning of their various expressions can be clarified by appropriate research.

The problem is that many researchers do not raise the initial questions of the literary form of the expression they intend to clarify.

role in carrying the teaching of the council forward.

It follows that before the investigation for finding the meaning of a term or expression is undertaken, the nature of that locution must be determined. If it is a straightforward affirmation, the work of construing its exact definition may well start immediately. If it is a seminal expression, it should be taken for such; it should be taken as a seed sown which must strike roots and grow branches before it can bear fruit. A seminal expression must be assimilated, pondered over before its potential meaning can unfold. Councils are entitled not only to make precise definitions but also to use an evangelical mode of speech.

Now we are able to come to the point: *obsequium* is one of these seminal words. The discussion whether it means precisely "respect" or "submission" works on a wrong assumption, which is that the council indeed meant it always in a specific and exact way. The council used many forms of speech.

When the council spoke of religious *obsequium* it meant an attitude toward the church which is rooted in the virtue of religion, the love of God and the love of his church. This attitude in every concrete case will be in need of further specification, which could be "respect", or could be "submission," depending on the progress the church has made in clarifying its own beliefs.[7]

---

[7]*See* especially LG 25 and DV 5.

Obsequium, like *communio,* ultimately signifies to be one with the church; one in mind and heart, which means one in belief and in action. *Obsequium* is a special expression of this communion, mainly in doctrinal matters. It is ideally perfect when someone is so well united in faith with the church that he or she believes all that the church holds firmly, and searches with the church when some point in our tradition is in need of clarification. In the first case we can speak of *obsequium fidei* (one with the believing church: holding firm to a doctrine), in the second case of an *obsequium religiosum* (one with the searching church, working for clarification).

To put it another way: the ongoing attempts to translate *obsequium* by one precise term are misguided efforts which originates in a lack of perception of the nature of that concept. *Obsequium* refers first to a general "attitude", not to any specific form of it. The external manifestation of a disposition can take many forms, depending on the person to whom *obsequium* must be rendered, or on the point of doctrine that is proposed as entitled to *obsequium.* Accordingly, the duty to offer *obsequium* may bind to respect, or to submission—or to any other attitude between the two.[8]

[8]The Italian word *ossequio* can also give a clue for the understanding of *obsequium:* every dictionary lists a whole gamut of English words in translating it; they range from "respect" to "submission" with many other attitudes in between. *Ossequio* really means a fundamental attitude which needs to take a specified concrete form, depending on the circumstances; in

When dissent is the response

Dissent has become one of the dominant themes in Catholic theology in the United States. As a rule, it means the refusal to accept some point of doctrine officially taught, but not infallibly defined. The right to such a dissent is vigorously vindicated by many theologians; there are also episcopal statements supporting it. To find a balance, efforts have been made to formulate guidelines for permissible dissent, and to assure that a "fair trial" is available should a conflict arise.

As far as I can ascertain it, dissent is mentioned less in European writings. Not that there are not any writers who dissent from the content of official documents; there are. But when they do, they tend to describe their approach as having an *opinion différente*, or being of *anderer Meinung*, and so forth. It may well be that the Europeans sense a problem with the word itself, and for that reason prefer to use other expressions.

In truth, dissent is an imperfect term under several aspects. When used it starts out on a negative note, indicating nothing positive. It is sweeping, with no recognizable boundaries. It could mean a purely intellectual

some cases it might be a polite expression of esteem, in other cases a manifestation of submission. A similar *type* of word in English would be "loyalty": it means an attitude which can be expressed in different ways—by loyal obedience or by loyal opposition.

stance, no more than a disagreement with the logic of a reasoning, or with the conclusion of a reflective process. But it could mean also an attitude of radical opposition to "the other side," ready to break the bond of unity, in which case the propositional disagreement is only an external sign of a deep-lying internal antagonism.[9]

No wonder the use of such an ill-defined word can easily provoke suspicion and negative reactions in the "other side". When this happens, the scene is set for a sharp conflict, and the best explanations may be lost in the swirling mist of emotions.[10]

Thus, "dissent" is too much of an ambivalent word, with too many existential connotations beyond a purely intellectual significance to be a useful term in theological

[9]The Oxford English Dictionary gives the following three definitions of a *dissenter*:

> 1. One who dissents in any matter; one who disagrees with any opinion, resolution, or proposal; a dissentient. 2. One who dissents and separates himself *from* any specified church or religious communion, especially from that which is historically the national church, or is in some way treated as such, or regarded as the orthodox body. 3. One who separates himself from the communion of the Established Church of England or (in Scotland) of Scotland.

[10]The language problems are not made easier by the fact that in political life a "dissenter" is often the one who is radically opposed to the ruling "establishment" and wants to get rid of it. Thus we speak of "dissenters" in totalitarian countries.

debates, which by definition are supposed to move on a rational level.

Besides, it is a historically loaded word, certainly in English. The term "dissenter" came into use in England in the seventeenth century. Originally it described those who intended to secede from the established church; later it was applied to those who had done so and formed the so-called free churches. Granted, today "to dissent" need not mean "to secede", but we should remember that words have a life of their own. They often continue to carry meanings which they have acquired in a distant past; no matter what the present speaker intends.

Attempts have been made also to define the "right" to dissent with some precision. The problem is, as those familiar with the internal workings of a legal system know, that such amorphous concepts are the least suitable for incorporation into a legal document, and if they are, they create situations unmanageable for the "rule of law." Any judge, wanting to uphold this right, would have to raise interminable questions: right to dissent from what? for what purpose? by what means? to what extent? in what precise circumstances? . . . and so on . . .! Rights are enforceable only when they are clearly defined, and their violation can be easily ascertained. If not, they open the door to endless litigations.[11]

---

[11]The First Amendment to the US Constitution wisely speaks of the "freedom of speech", and by implication the right to free speech. Difficult

It follows that if we abandoned the word "dissent" altogether, we would lose little and gain much. If we could get into the habit of speaking of a researcher as holding another opinion or having come to a different conclusion or proposing a diverse hypothesis, we would only tell the truth positively. After all, hardly ever does a theologian dissent from a proposal and then settle down in a no-man's-land without an opinion; he dissents precisely because he has reached a positive conclusion, but a different one. If so, he might as well say it. Moreover, attitudinally, he may not be dissenting at all; rather, he many be consenting wholeheartedly to the search for a better understanding of the Christian mysteries.

All these arguments notwithstanding, it appears that for the time being at least, not only must we live with an unsuitable word, but we have to assert the legitimate right of the faithful to scientific research and to a different opinion through the use of a confusing expression: "the right to dissent." So be it.

How to determine the limits of legitimate dissent?

As soon as this query is raised, all the latent ambiguities of the term surface—with a vengance. What kind of

as it is for the courts to adjudicate cases concerning that right, how much greater their burden would be if they had to adjudicate "freedom of dissent" and the right to free dissent!

dissent are we talking about? Dissent from what? For what purpose? And so forth. Please, Reader, bear with the complexities, it comes from the subject matter, not from the writer. There has been already too much simplification concerning this issue; the penalty for continuing with it would be severe: confusion would reign supreme.[12]

At any rate, here and now we are seeking the permissible limits of a propositional dissent. That is, we assume that the dissenter has surrendered to God who reveals himself, and that he has accepted the Catholic belief concerning the role of the church in guarding and proclaiming the evangelical message. We are talking about

---

[12]Yves Congar in his *Vrai et fausse réforme dans l'Eglise* gives a set of rules for what a *contestation* must never do, in order to avoid being destructive of the church. *Mutatis mutandis,* the rules can point to the limits of dissent. He writes:

> In the church *la contestation* can never be: (1) destructive of charity, . . . activity that wounds the heart; . . . (2) a calling in question of those hierarchical pastoral structures of the church for which the foundations were laid by the Lord; . . . (3) the denial or the calling in question, in a hasty, thoughtless and irresponsible fashion, of those points of doctrine for which one should rather sacrifice one's life; . . . (4) a rejection of those who think otherwise as bad persons, irretrievably lost; regarding them as damned without hope; . . . (5) one cannot admit expressions of *contestation* in a liturgical celebration, for instance, in the homily. This would create an unbearable climate of tension and agitation in the assembly. Whatever we may think, the others have a right to peace and to respect for their position. (*See* p. 518)

a dissenter who is in full communion with the Catholic *ecclesia.*

That is, we assume that he consents to the core of the Catholic belief as it has been handed down by the church from generation to generation, confirmed and affirmed by the great councils, or by the pope speaking with that infallibility with which Christ wanted his church to be endowed (cf. Vatican Council I).[13]

Now, here is the question: In such circumstances, could the legitimacy of the dissent be decided by invoking the distinction between infallible and non-infallible teaching, and saying that dissent from non-infallibly defined propositions is legitimate?

The answer cannot be a simple *yes* because of the complex composition of the *corpus* of non-infallible beliefs and opinions; that *corpus,* as we have seen earlier in this book, may contain much that belongs to the core of our tradition but which (as yet) has not become the object of an infallible "determination."

A historical illustration can show the correctness of this statement. The Reformers of the sixteenth century dis-

---

[13]Because of a widely spread contrary opinion, it remains necessary to stress (and repeat) that the primary subject of infallibility is *the church,* not the pope, not the episcopal college. Here is the text of Vatican Council I:

> The Roman Pontiff . . . enjoys the infallibility with which the divine Redeemer wanted his church to be endowed in defining doctrine concerning faith or morals. (DS 3074)

sented from traditional beliefs on many points which were in no way infallibly defined at that time (not even the seven sacraments were defined!). Yet, as it turned out, they were wrong; in some instances, their denial went against the core of our tradition. Part of the message of the Council of Trent is that someone *may be* breaking the unity of faith even if the doctrine denied has never been the object of a conciliar definition.

The situation is not all that different today. In the non-infallible corpus there are surely "seeds of truth" which in due course will enter into the core known with infallible knowledge. Therefore, to state simply that dissent from non-infallibly held doctrine is legitimate, is simplistic and incorrect. Before any judgment is made, the relationship of the non-infallible doctrine to the infallible core ought to be examined, and then a judicious statement should be made whether or not an act of dissent is permissible or not.[14]

A good theologian should be able to perceive the standing of a particular point of doctrine in the process of developing; he responds accordingly. He knows that before

[14]Doctrines are defined because they belong to the core of the Christian tradition (that is, they are not added to the core because they were defined). The definition itself is an external authentication of an internal unity. It follows that when a point of doctrine is questioned and dissent is intended, the prospective dissenter must always move beyond the issue of "it-has-not-been-defined-infallibly" and ask what is the relationship of the contested doctrine to the core of the tradition.

the doctrine reaches full maturity and can be affirmed with an act of faith, there is a long process. The pronouncements by popes and bishops have their own place in this movement. They benefit from an assistance of the Spirit, not only to determine (when the times are ripe for it) with finality what the church must believe but also to promote the progress of such belief.

Their contribution , however, should leave plenty of room for the theologians. Ideally, the two (hierarchy and theologians) should work in harmony; when they do, the results are likely to be enlightenment, peace and harmony (as happened at Vatican II). If they do not, conflicts are inevitable (as is happening in our times).[15]

[15]The success of Vatican Council II was due as much to the insights of the theologians as to the judgment s of the bishops. It was an ideally construed situation for progress. To begin with, the theologians were trusted; they were officially invited to contribute. They came not only from all places, but from all schools of thought. They did much of the work by themselves; then they put their insights before commissions composed of theologians and bishops who did much of the screening, selecting and deciding what should be put before the plenary assembly. Finally, the bishops voted at their general congregations. Throughout it all there was a balanced play. The daring insights (or the pedestrian thinking) of the theologians were subject to the "Christian common sense" approach of the bishops; that is, intellectual discourses were measured by pastoral effectiveness. The final documents are the results of such a play, which was both creative and moderating.

If only such conditions could be recreated in the church of today, much of our woes would disappear. The thinkers in the church need the sobering influence of the pastors, and the pastors need the refreshing influence of the thinkers. At bottom, our problem is that we are still reluctant to accept the

In this process,the voice of a theologian who remains in communion but proposes an answer different from the one given by those in authority may not be an act of dissent at all; rather, it may be a needed contribution to the development of doctrine, coming from someone who is assenting to every part of the revealed truth but is in the process of searching for the whole truth.

Should there be guidelines for dissent?

There have been many attempts to set up precise guidelines for handling dissent but really no rules can cover every single case. Ultimately there is no substitute for the learning, prudence and wisdom of those who are involved in the case.[16]

fact that the church is a *community* where nothing will go well unless we act as a community. Theologians and bishops had many disagreements during Heenan, Archbishop of Westminster: *Timeo peritos annexa ferentes,* "I fear the experts bringing their *addenda!*"?); yet, intent on serving the church, they were forged into a community by the events of the council. Such a close and intimate cooperation can never be achieved through occasional contacts.

[16]Concerning the non-infallible magisterium, the German episcopate in a "working paper" (for the internal use of their conference?) dated September 22, 1967 (that is, before *Humanae vitae*) acknowledged that

> . . . it is a fact that the teaching authority of the church in the exercise of its office can make mistakes and has made mistakes. The church has always known that such occurrences are

The hierarchy should certainly do everything to maintain a favorable climate for creative work; the church needs it. This includes generous trust in the persons who do the work of research and reflection; they should be allowed a reasonable margin for honest mistakes. After all, who would ever join a research team on the condition that no mistaken hypothesis can ever be proposed?![17] Besides,

possible, kept stating it in its theology, and has provided guidance for handling such situations.

Obviously dissent from such mistakes cannot be wrong.

To my best knowledge this paper has never been officially published but has been widely quoted; Karl Rahner commented on it. My reference is Hans Waldenfels "Von der Sprachnot in der Kirche" in *Stimmen der Zeit* 112 (1987), pp. 222-223.

The bishops of the United States allowed dissent from non-infallible teaching provided there is no attack on the teaching authority itself and no "scandal" is caused among the faithful. See in *Human Life in Our Day: A Collective Pastoral Letter of the American Hierarchy* (Washington, DC: USCC, 1968).

[17]It belongs to the very essence of research that on the basis of the data available various working hypotheses are proposed; then, each is checked out to see that it covers the facts to be explained but does not go beyond them. Under this aspect, theological research is not different; as a rule, the right hypothesis is found only after a number of incorrect ones have been discarded. But how could they be discarded, unless they were proposed? Aquinas rejected the hypothesis of the immaculate conception because for him it contradicted the dogma of original sin; Duns Scotus retained the doctrine of immaculate conception because he found a way of reconciling it with the belief in original sin. In more modern times, Pius XII in his encyclical *Humani generis* condemned the doctrine of polygenesis (as applied to the human race) because it did not appear how such a theory could be "composed" with the traditional teaching about the transmission

the church is strong enough to bear with some dissenting elements.

The researchers can help to create this climate if they are aware of their own limits; that is, if they have a good perception of how much they do not know. To claim that theologians should be left alone and ultimately be subject to correction by their peers only ignores the warnings of history: all too many times in our Christian past "faculties of theology" in various universities have been wrong altogether.[18] Besides, if such a claim were taken literally, it

of original sin; but by saying so he left the door open to the acceptance of polygenesis as soon as there is a hypothesis which can harmonize it with the tradition that we all are born with original sin (cf. DS 3897). Since then several such hypotheses have been proposed although none of them succeeded in winning the consensus of theologians.

The main point here is simple: there is no progress in any science, theology included, unless there is enough room for hypotheses to be proposed and to be discarded. Presumably, the more the merrier—within reason.

For some mysterious reason, there is a widespread intolerance toward theologians: they are expected to come up with the correct solution, to be right the first time!

To be fair to all sides, the theologians too have to abide by the rules of this game; never on any account should they call a hypothesis the final truth.

[18]The faculty of the University of Paris helped to provide the "justification" for the condemnation of Joan of Arc. Cf. Regine Pernoud & M.-V. Clin, *Jeanne d'Arc*, (Paris: Fayard, 1986), pp. 167-169. The theologians of the same university also provided leaders and arguments for the movement of extreme conciliarism in the 15th century.

would imply that the theologians have the assistance of the Spirit to decide ultimately cases of conflict in doctrinal matters. I do not think that either *Magister Gratianus* or *Frater Thomas* would have accepted that.

Thus, to maintain a climate for creativity and to do creative work is a fine balancing act; the result of many prudential judgments. The best one can say is that when a concrete case presents itself, it must be judged on its own merits—and those merits may significantly differ from one case to another. This is not to say that there should be no guidelines, but it is to say that not too much trust should be put into the guidelines.

The charism of the bishops and the task of the theologians

The crux of the problem is in the fact that the bishops' charism, sustained by the Spirit, at least when they act in unity, is *to witness* God's mighty deeds: "You are witnesses

"When the famous scholar and poet Fray Luis de Leon was arrested in 1572 [by the Spanish Inquisition], he succeeded in identifying some of his accusers by the simple means of naming most of his colleagues at the University of Salamanca as possible personal enemies; . . ." Quote from Cecil Roth, *The Spanish Inquisition*, (New York: Norton, 1964), p. 89. Eventually, after some years in prison, he was acquitted.

The time of the Reformation both on the Continent and in England could provide ample examples of vacillations and tergiversations by "Faculties of Theology."

of these things" (Luke 24:48).[19] The gift and task of the theologians is *to find deeper insights: intellegere;* that is, *interlegere,* to read what is not obvious, to find hidden meanings.[20] To witness is to identify; to identify is not necessarily to read in depth. To have the intelligence to find hidden meanings does not necessarily imply the support of the Spirit for identifying God's deeds.

From the point of view of epistemology it would make good sense to say that the primary focus of the bishops is *to affirm the existence* of the mysteries, the principal concentration of the theologians is *to penetrate the meaning* of the

---

[19]A good definition of witnessing is "to testify that a thing is"; cf. *Oxford Greek Dictionary,* under *martureo,* n. 5, in order to remain close to the biblical language. But the same sense is found in the *Oxford English Dictionary* under *witness:* "attestation of a fact, event, or statement," also "one who gives evidence in relation to matters of fact."

[20]The task of the theologian can be beautifully described by quoting the meanings of *intellegere* as they are listed in the *Oxford Latin Dictionary;* all that one has to do is to refer the various mental activities to the Christian mysteries:

> To grasp mentally, understand, realize; . . .
> To understand by inference, deduce. . . . to supply
>   mentally, understand (something that is not expressed).
> To discern, recognize, . . . to distinguish mentally,
>   recognize as existing.
> To understand the value of, appreciate.
> To understand the meaning of (words or languages) . . .
> To have or exercise powers of understanding.

same mysteries as much as possible.[21] Obviously this is no more than a philosophical approximation to a reality which in many ways is beyond the reach of philosophy; still, it may shed some light on it.[22]

[21]This distinction, I think, is helpful for the understanding of the different functions, but it should not be pushed too far. No bishop can affirm the existence of the Christian mysteries without explaining their meaning, which always presupposes a certain amount of reflection. But the scientific (systematic and critical) exploration of the mysteries is not likely to be the primary focus of a bishop in his pastoral activity; he himself would regard it as a task better left to the theologians.

The theologians must rely on the testimony of the bishops about the word of God; the bishops may receive enlightenment from the systematic and critical work of the theologians.

Without the testimony of the bishops the theologians could not be certain what the word of God is; without the accumulated wisdom of theologians the bishop would know less about the meaning of the Word.

[22]There have been many attempts to draw up rules and regulations that could help to resolve conflicts between bishops and theologians. Such rules, however, can offer hardly more than a limited service. *First,* because no norms can be so perfect as to anticipate the great variety of cases that are bound to arise; *second,* because the norms are regularly construed on the assumption that the conflicts originate in conceptual differences which can be resolved by appropriate logical exchanges—dialogues, that is.

In reality, the conflicts often originate on a deeper level: in the difference between the episcopal calling and the theological enterprise. Bishops are called (and have the charism) to witness to an existential fact: Christ *is* risen; the theologians are called (and have the learning) to give a reflective explanation of this fact: the resurrection *means*. . . It is easy to see that the one who proclaims the fact may become concerned that the other may explain it away; especially if the explanation cannot be easily understood.

Then there is the problem of bishops and theologians operating within different horizons (an epistemological issue that deserves more attention

Dissent in the existential order

The difficulties would end here, were we living in a world (or a church) which is ruled by conceptual propositions and nothing else. But the real world is quite different. It is also a world of strong emotional dynamics and irrational options. All dissents, no matter how propositional, operate in such a world.

Moreover, those who are entrusted with the pastoral care of the community must take into account not only the intellectual propositions and exchanges, but also the waves they cause in the turbulent universe of human beings.

Thus, two more situations ought to be mentioned. One is when the propositional dissent of a theologian (without his ever intending it) in fact becomes a feeder to a deeper

than it gets). Now, horizons can never be bridged by dialogues alone; since the meaning of a word depends not only on its content but on its place within a given horizon. (The same word can carry different meanings in different horizons.) If the parties in dialogue are not aware of this fact, at most, there will be endless talks coupled with polite tolerance but no meeting of minds and hearts. The passage from one horizon into another cannot be achieved by a new conceptual understanding; it is the surrender of the whole person to a new environment. Thomas Aquinas entered into the horizon of Aristotelian philosophy, and found new meanings in traditional Christian concepts. Etienne Tempier, the bishop of Paris, and the two successive Archbishops of Canterbury, Robert Kilwardby and John Peckham could never follow him—so they condemned or attacked him. I doubt any "dialogue" between the theologian and his hierarchical adversaries would have helped; only an intellectual conversion of the bishops could have brought mutual understanding and reconciliation.

attitudinal dissent in others. I am not thinking here of causing a childish scandal, or of provoking a hypocritical protest on the part of those who cultivate their ignorance. I am speaking of concrete situations where the peace or unity of the church for some reason is seriously threatened, and, as a matter of fact, a reasonable act of dissent when perceived by others feeds into the dynamics of disruption and fragmentation. This is by no means a figment of imagination; for instance, in a country where there is an ongoing effort by the government to tear the church apart, a most legitimate act of disagreement may promote the disintegration of the community. Clearly, in such cases more is at stake than a propositional dissent; prudence requires a judgment that takes into account the existential situation of the community.

Another such a situation is when the propositional dissent itself springs from an internal breach of communion, or moves towards it; if that happens the issue is a much deeper one and eventually may cause serious disruptions in the community. If there is a remedy it is in a reconciliation on an equally deep level.

Practical examples

After these theoretical reflections, let some practical examples speak for themselves.

(1) Let us assume for the sake of argument that the

proposition "A sacramental and consummated marriage is indissoluble" is not infallibly defined (some theologians hold that it is, some hold that it is not). The ordinary official documents of the church certainly speak of it as indissoluble.

There comes a theologian who declares his dissent from the official teaching. The reaction of those in authority is a declaration that the person must not be taken for a Catholic theologian. How to judge this case?

The theologian should clarify his position further. If he means that the church has some radical power, in virtue of the power of the keys, to dissolve sacramental marriages, even consummated, but does not wish to use it in order to protect the common good, he would be saying only what has been said intermittently in the course of history (even at the Council of Trent) and is part of the teaching of the Orthodox church. If he means that any couple at any time can dissolve their marriage on their own authority and be free to wed again, then our theologian is contradicting a virtually uninterrupted tradition in the East and in the West; consequently, his opinion is at variance with the Catholic doctrine.

If the conflict between the theologian and the proper authority develops without the necessary subtle clarifications, the conflict is misplaced; it has erupted before the issues were properly defined. From such a conflict no light is likely to emerge.

(2) Let us suppose, again for the sake of argument, that in a given country abortions abound and they are on the rise. A theologian gets hold of the writings of Aquinas and finds the doctrine that the "animation" of the fetus occurs several weeks after its conception. From there he concludes and proclaims that the termination of pregnancy is permissible, provided it takes place before the animation. (The church never defined the time of animation.)

Yes, but there are other not so rational factors playing their part. Few of the citizens would be able to appreciate the philosophical *finesse* of the theory of Aquinas, or perceive how ill-suited his ideas are to explain the discoveries of modern biology. In the concrete order the argument of the theologian would simply add to the dynamics of the movement for abortions.

Have the ecclesiastical authorities the right to intervene, in spite of the fact that no infallible doctrine is denied? It seems that the authorities have the duty to intervene because the seemingly innocent theory feeds powerfully into the forces of destruction. The object of the pastoral care of the church is the concrete existential order of the world.

These examples should confirm what has been said before: whenever a concrete case of "dissent" presents itself, there is no one standard solution that can be applied with precision. We certainly have enough general principles to work with, but there are also particular circumstances, which make every case unique. It follows that the practical resolution of an individual case can come only through a unique prudential judgment. The way to such a judgment is through an effort to discover the correct hierarchy of values in the concrete circumstances of the case, and then do what is necessary to support the more important ones.

It is good to recall, however, that because our knowledge in assessing the objective facts and in judging the words and deeds of a person is always limited, most prudential judgments are not perfect; they are subject to correction, should new information reach us or should we come to better insights. Thus, in ordinary circumstances the zeal for the purity of the house of God should be tempered with the awareness of human fallibility.

*

With this the section on the response of the people is concluded.

In the following and last part I shall examine the role of the Catholic universities, since so much of the interplay between the teaching authority and the theological community takes place there.

4

TEACHING AUTHORITY
CATHOLIC UNIVERSITIES
ACADEMIC FREEDOM

In our contemporary world Catholic universities occupy
a special position in the intellectual life of the church. Since
most of the work of the theologians is done there, both in
research and in teaching, universities have a mediating role
in the interplay between the magisterium and the community at large, besides mediating between the evangelical
message and the local culture. This essay, therefore, would
not be complete without a brief description and assessment
of their structures and operations, and in particular of the
various types of relationships they can establish with the
believing community in general and with the teaching
authority in particular.

My main purpose in this section is to present a reasoned
understanding of how a university can be Catholic, and,
once Catholic, how its life can be receptive and responsive
to the pronouncements of the magisterium. Sound method

and logic postulate, however, that before we speak of how a university can have a religious dimension, the very idea of university should be clarified.

The house of intellect

The starting point of our reflection should be a fact: universities are of human creation.[1] They are the products

---

[1]First an acknowledgement: I have been inspired to use the expression "house of intellect" by Barzun (see Bibliography).

What follows is clearly a summary description; but that is all we need to come to a good and operational understanding of what a Catholic university can be and how it ought to function. The analysis offered is applicable to other Catholic institutions, such as hospitals, social works, etc. At the basis of this theory there are some simple assumptions: the humanity of an institution should be affirmed and respected; the freedom of such human institutions to develop a religious dimension should be upheld; the freedom of the church to reach out for human institutions and establish various degrees of association or union with them should be recognized. It is this analysis that opens the vista for a legitimate pluralism in creating specifically Catholic institutions. (I am very much aware also of the fact that there are countries where the Catholic community has not, and does not, favor the establishment of Catholic universities.)

It would be beyond the scope of this essay to quote documents and statements concerning the nature of a university and in particular of academic freedom, issued by various societies and associations, such as the International Federation of Catholic Universities, American Association of University Professors, Canon Law Society of America jointly with the Catholic Theological Society of America, and others; they are easily available elsewhere (for references see Hansel, Kaplin, Sullivan in the Bibliography).

of a long and complex cultural evolution; they are also marked by the particular traditions and customs of the nation to which they belong.[2] But no matter how different they may be from one country to another, there is a common denominator that sets them apart from all other institutions: they are the "houses of intellect." They are specialized establishments with the purpose of supporting and promoting the operations of the human mind in acquiring and communicating knowledge. They play a particular role in the complex machinery of the human society, not unlike the way the mind plays a particular role in the human person. If their relationship with the social body is not balanced, both sides suffer. An isolated university (an ivory tower that stands alone) is bound to become a useless eyesore; a university that loses its identity (it dissolves into a political or social action group) leaves the whole community intellectually weak and undernourished. Obviously, I am not suggesting that there cannot be intellectual life outside the universities (it would be silly even to think so); I am simply stating that much of the advancement in learning and in the communication of knowledge in our culture takes place within the universities.

[2]For the history of universities in a nutshell, with as many details squeezed in as such a shell can hold, see A. Franzen "Universitaeten" in LTK, 10: 510-517. The name was first used in 1221 by the masters and students of Paris: *nos universitas magistrorum et scolarium.*

The inside operations of a university consist principally in gathering data, reflecting on them, searching for the laws that govern them, always with the view of communicating the information and intelligence so acquired to generations of students. Throughout it all, good teachers will know that there is more to a person than the operations of the mind, therefore they will function and present their instructions in a broader context which takes into account the needs of the whole human person and of the human family at large.

In performing their multiple task, universities may specialize further. Some will put more emphasis on research, catering mainly to graduate students; others will perform best in teaching and training undergraduates; again, some may develop adult education programs in the service of the larger communities around them. Such diversification is legitimate; each university should have the right to shape its own life and destiny—as long as it remains the house of intellect. Beyond that, theoretical discussions as to what "a university as such" or "by its essence" ought to be, may become idle speculation with little relevance to reality. Universities exist in the concrete order only. Each community has its own needs, and its own potential.

Much is said today about the duty of every university to be value-oriented. No one should quarrel with such a statement; in fact, it is difficult to see how any institution of higher learning could ever function without being value-oriented; after all, the possession of knowledge and the spreading of it are very much values in themselves. The issue is rather about what values a university should serve and promote in choosing its fields of research, in educating the citizens, and also in inserting itself into the life of the civic community.[3]

Catholic universities, while intending to remain universities, have chosen an orientation toward religious values.

When is a university Catholic?

Let us begin at the simplest and most obvious test: When is the adjective "Catholic" used for a "university"? Clearly, when people perceive some kind of connection or association between a university and the Catholic com-

---

[3]As a rule, the claim that the university should be value-oriented refers to orientation toward moral values. It means that the university should provide instructions for learning about values, help the students to develop a critical capacity to judge values and provide them with sound criteria for making moral decisions. It is easier said than done. The problem is that the acceptance of a value system is very much of a personal option. A "house of intellect" can certainly present the options; moreover, it can provide inspiration, e.g., by effectively upholding basic human rights on campus, by promoting international cooperation for the peaceful resolution of conflicts, etc. If the institution is religiously committed, its life and operations will be permeated by religious values, which in itself is the presentation of an option.

munity. Not much investigation is required to notice that this use of the term can cover a great variety of situations.

Those situations, however, are not so disparate that they could not be classified into a few types, each displaying a different kind of structural link between a university and the believing community. I shall list six of them, moving from the loosest of relationships to the closest of unions. Please note that these models are not mere conceptual constructs but they represent concrete situations. They are typified images leaving aside many individual variations. After the description of each I shall add also a short note about their position in canon law.

1. Secular universities in a Catholic environment

There are universities, established and operated by a secular authority, but within an environment where the Catholic influence is strong. Inevitably, the religious beliefs of the persons on campus, faculty, students, administrators, will have some impact on the operation of the institution itself. As a rule, the name Catholic would not be applied to such institutions; or very loosely, to distinguish them from other universities attended principally by non-Catholics. In this sense the National University in Dublin was called, in less ecumenical times, a Catholic university, in distinction from Trinity College which was spoken of as a Protestant institution.

Canon law has no competency in this case.

2. *Secular universities integrated with a Catholic academic unit*

There are secular universities with confessionally dedicated theology departments. Such universities are not referred to as religious, but their academic units are known under the name of the church which sponsors them. Thus, in Germany, Austria and Switzerland there are state universities with Catholic or Evangelical or Reformed "faculties" of theology.

> Virtually all such Catholic "faculties" have their special statutes approved by the ecclesiastical authorities within the framework of a concordat between the civil government and the Holy See.

3. *Universities nourished by Catholic tradition but with no formal institutional commitment*

There are universities, officially classified as non-denominational (non-sectarian), but which were founded under Catholic auspices and are operating strongly within that tradition. Although in their institutional structures they do not reflect any religious commitment, they assert their fidelity to a living tradition, and their various constituencies *de facto* keep the Catholic ideals alive, as a free choice on their part.[4] Such Catholic universities can be found in the United States and Canada.

[4]The reason for not inserting any religious commitment into the charter or by-laws of some traditionally Catholic universities is usually in the civil law system within which they must operate. A legal tie with a religious

Such universities exist and operate outside of the canonical structures. Since the church asserts a "proprietary" right over the term "Catholic," if they want to use it in their name, they must petition for a "license."

4. *Universities with institutional commitment to Catholic ideals but without an ecclesiastical charter*

There are universities which by their own decision wanted to commit themselves to the pursuit of truth within the context of Catholic ideals. To assure this orientation, they inserted into their statutes significant provisions to the same effect: e.g. some members of the board must represent a religious community, the President must be Catholic, and similar ones. They have not, however, petitioned for an ecclesiastical charter, hence they have not become "persons" in canon law; they are not (as an institution) under the jurisdiction of the Holy See or of the local ordinary.[5] Still,

---

denomination would civilly disadvantage them to the point that they could be compelled to close down altogether; which is a good illustration of the thesis that no amount of abstract reasoning can decide what is the best way for a university to be Catholic. If what is theoretically the best may lead practically the worst, less perfect ways must be found to uphold and support Christian values in a secular society.

Such universities can prosper as Catholic institutions only if all its constituencies (faculty, students, administration, alumni, benefactors, etc.) freely support their orientation. This is true, of course, of the next category as well.

[5]This does not mean that the Catholic persons working at such universities are not under the jurisdiction of the ecclesiastical authorities.

they wish a close relationship with the church, a "communion" built on mutual respect and trust. Rightly, they describe themselves as Catholic universities, although as a rule without using that adjective in their name. Often they are closely associated with, or supported by, an institute of consecrated life or a society of apostolic life. This type is mostly found in the United States.

The same as above.

5. *Universities established by the church with a canonical charter*

There are "Catholic universities" which are incorporated into the legal structures of the church. In canon law they have a juridical personality, accordingly they are subjects of rights and duties. They are, as an institution, under the jurisdiction of the Holy See (and of the local bishop, or of a committee of bishops, as the case may be); they report to the Congregation for Catholic Education and they have a

They are *as individuals*. This distinction becomes very important for deciding how issues of church discipline must be handled, should they ever arise. On the level of law, either the Holy See or the local ordinary ought to contact directly the person concerned.

There is no other correct approach in canon law. Unless an institution obtains legal personality in the church, it cannot have legal rights and duties in the church.

It is a different question whether or not an institution which professes itself Catholic is *morally* bound to take action against a member who publicly displays a destructive behavior against the religious commitment of the university. There is no *a priori* answer to this question; it is a matter for prudential judgment. More of this later in the text.

standing before an ecclesiastical court. Their assets are ecclesiastical goods, normally subject to the canonical rules of acquisition and alienation. They need not have an exclusive or even primary orientation toward the "sacred sciences." The degrees they confer, although recognized by the church, may simply follow the civil pattern customary in the country. All such details are handled in their church-approved statutes. The Catholic universities of Leuven and of Louvain-la-Neuve fall into this category; also The Catholic University of America.

> The canonical status, the rights and duties, of such universities are regulated in the Code of Canon Law; see the chapter on "Catholic Universities and Other Institutes of Higher Studies"; canons 807-814.

6. "Ecclesiastical Universities and Faculties" established by the church and dedicated to "sacred sciences"

There are "Ecclesiastical Universities and Faculties" specifically founded by the authority of the Holy See and under the direction of the same. Their main purpose is to do research in the field of "sacred sciences" (such as biblical studies, church history, theology, canon law, etc.) and to teach them in a scientific manner. They confer ecclesiastical degrees with canonical effects. They are juridical persons in the church, with corresponding rights and duties. Their establishment and operations are regulated by an apostolic constitution, *Sapientia christiana*, which requires each to present its own statutes for approval. *De facto* most of such institutions are instrumental also in training candidates for ordination. The Pontifical Universities in Rome (Gregorian, Lateran, St. Thomas and others), the specifically "ecclesiastical faculties" (Theology, Canon Law and Philosophy) of The Catholic University of America are good examples for this category.

> For the applicable laws see the chapter in the Code of Canon Law on "Ecclesiastical Universities and Faculties"; canons 815-821 and the Apostolic Constitution *Sapientia Christiana,* promulgated April 15, 1979, and the subsequent *Ordinationes* by the Congregation for Catholic Education, promulgated April 29, 1979.

These are six typical situations, but to know them for what they are a few more remarks must be added.

*The dividing lines between the different types cannot be always sharply drawn. At times, their individual variations are such that they blend into each other; this may especially occur between the first and second, the third and fourth, and the fifth and sixth categories.

*When it is a question of assessing the Catholic character of a university, it is never enough to ask about the structures of its organization; such as how many courses on religion are offered, whether or not certain offices are reserved for Catholics, etc.; it is necessary also to inquire about the internal dynamics operating in the institution. The forces which create and sustain the religious commitment of an institution are never immobile and unchanging (no less than in a human person); in the real world such an energy is either increasing in intensity, or decreasing in vitality. To observe such a movement over a longer period of time is just as important as to know the structures.

It is quite possible that two institutions exhibit the same static pattern today, but underneath they are moved by opposite forces. The full impact of those internal currents will be revealed only in, say, fifty years, when one will be a strong and healthy Catholic institution, the other a respectable seat of learning but without any religious orientation.

*The intensity of religious dedication should be always distinguished from legal structures and corporate charters. High-sounding statutory statements may not cover deep convictions, and vice versa, deep convictions may be present even if there are no legally sanctioned expressions.

*There is nothing, absolutely nothing, in any of the six types that would be objectionable from a Catholic theological point of view. All are honest and respectable combinations of academic life and religious dedication. The question, however, *which must be raised,* is whether or not a given combination is the best (the most prudent, the most efficient) way of upholding human and religious values in a given place and at a given time.

Thus, it may not be wise to push for a canonically

chartered Catholic university at a place where public universities operate in a Christian spirit within a Christian climate.

Also, it may not be wise to compel Catholic universities which operate freely and vigorously in a secular society to enter into a legal bond with the church if by this act they become so disadvantaged civilly that they lose their position and must reduce their service to the community.[6]

But it may be wise for a Catholic institution in a country with an oppressive government to obtain a legal charter from the Holy See and secure the protection that canon law can give in order to be free from interference by the state.[7]

---

[6]This would be a typical case of losing concrete values in the real order for the sake of abstract values conceived in the abstract order.

[7]At times one hears the statement: the mind of the church is that to be Catholic a university must be under the jurisdiction of the ecclesiastical authorities. I doubt that such could be the mind of the church. In all likelihood the church would be *very* glad to have Catholic institutions of the third and fourth type (bond of communion with the church, but no legal tie) in countries where the official policy of the government is to propagate and support atheism. The mind of the church would be to take full advantage of the freedom granted. No responsible person in the church would disavow such institutions because they do not have a canonical charter; their support from the hierarchy would be overwhelming.

Catholic university defined by its purpose

After this brief look at the empirical reality of the Catholic universities, we should be in position to raise the question: What is a Catholic university? Or: How ought a university to be if it wants to be Catholic? Or: What makes a university Catholic? [8]

We are no longer seeking an empirical answer, we want a critically sustainable definition or determination which can serve as a guideline for both the founding of Catholic universities and the assessment of the operation of the existing ones. But how to proceed? If past discussions are of any guide, they tell us that the path toward this determination can be full of pitfalls, either leading into a maze of endless discussions, or into the temptation to jump to conclusions. Caution is necessary.

A good starting point is to make clear that a university is not some kind of metaphysical substance from which its "essential definition" can be deduced. It is ultimately a complex structure of human operations, a set of relationships built upon characteristic activities; all of them ordered to a specific end. *In this end is the clue for determining*

---

[8]The answer to this last question is: *people*. This is to anticipate the gist of a conclusion to come; also to stress right from the beginning that ultimately *persons*, and persons alone can make a university Catholic. (But please, do not conclude that the mere presence of persons is enough!)

what a university is in general, and what a Catholic university is in particular.[9]

At this point we are at a critical juncture; our inquiry could go in two different directions. One leads into the world of abstractions, the other into the world of concrete realities.

Let us see what happens in each case.

If someone takes the path into the world of abstractions, he will raise the question about how the best values, to their highest degree, can be obtained by a university. That is, he will focus his attention on an ideal end, construed mentally. It should not be difficult for him to find an answer. From there is just one logical step to the definition of *the* Catholic university. Once he is in possession of that definition, he has the criterion to judge and to evaluate, with a certainty that only metaphysics (possibly combined with religious conviction) can give, all other definitions and all universities.[10] The problem with this method is that

---

[9]In scholastic terms: the correct definition of university comes from its *causa finalis*, not from its *causa materialis* or *formalis*. This is not mere playing with words; it touches the heart of the matter.

It follows that if the question "What is the essence of a Catholic university"refers to a mysterious substance in the institution, it is a misconceived and misdirected question. If it refers to the purpose of the university, it is a good question and leads to the correct answer; such as: it is of the essence of a Catholic university that its operations are directed toward the realization of Catholic values.

[10]This was the way Plato conceived and worked out the constitutions of his ideal state, which no one, not even himself, could ever put into practice.

the inquirer went out of the real world, and his conclusions are applicable only in an ideal world. Abstract values are no more real than abstract mountains, and abstract values are no more attainable than abstract mountains are climbable. The other path is into the world of concrete realities. This *is* the correct path because it leads to real values, which can exist in the concrete world only. Therefore, the right question in every single instance when a Catholic university is to be founded or being evaluated is a prudential (that is, practical as distinct from metaphysical) question: What type of bond between the secular reality of a university and the sacred aspirations of a religious community is most suitable (most conducive to the realization of values) in a given place at a given time?

The world in which a university must take its place and carry out its operations is by no means uniform; it is full of differences originating in the mentality of the local people, their culture, their civil laws, their very perception of a university. In such an uneven world there is no uniform way of fostering values. The answer cannot be but a prudential judgment.[11] But let me add immediately, there is a duty to reach for the very best obtainable values in the circumstances; there is no virtue in a shallow compromise.[12]

[11]That is a judgment which goes beyond the abstract perception of values and takes into account the concrete and particular circumstances.

[12]Our approach is not mere pragmatism either. Admittedly, the judgment about what values are attainable in the practical order is a

Thus a Catholic university can blend in the best sense of the term into its environment, it can be the salt of the earth, or better, it can be the well-measured leaven in the mass. (If the leaven is not judiciously measured, either it remains ineffective or spoils the mass.)

Further, because a prudential judgment by its very nature is about concrete situations, the persons best qualified to make it are the persons fully familiar with the circumstances. Without their knowledge, notional and experiential, an abstract theory can be construed, but a feasible plan cannot be worked out.

Let us collect now the fragments of these terse reasonings, and (I submit) there emerges a balanced and harmonious image of what a Catholic university ought to be.

It is the house of intellect made all the brighter by the light of faith. More prosaically, it is an institution to uphold and promote human and religious values according to Catholic beliefs.

It is well-proportioned to its environment; it is adapted to its neighborhood; it blends into the social structures of the place. It provides as much opportuinity for the advancement of learning and religion as possible at a given moment of history. For its religious dedication, it relies primarily on the internal disposition of its constituencies; it

pragmatic one; but the judgment about what values are the true and authentic ones can be based only on sound philosophy or religious faith.

is part and member of the Catholic communion but it uses a canonical framework as far as it is helpful in promoting its primary end.

Because the circumstances in which Catholic universities must fulfill their end vary, there is a great deal of variation in their structures and operations; rightly so. The task of the ecclesiastical authorities is to respect this natural order of things and to encourage such a variety. The temptation for the authorities may be to proceed in an abstract way, and to judge the concrete good by the abstract best. Once such a judgment is formed, and the necessary power of jurisdiction is at hand, it takes just one step to make "the ideal" into a common legal norm. If that happens, true values may be the victims. An attempt to impose forcibly what is the best in the abstract but unsuitable in the concrete circumstances, can destroy quickly what good and prudent persons succeeded in building over a long period of time.[13]

---

[13]The first canon on "Catholic Universities" in the Code of Canon Law begins: "The church has the right to establish and to direct universities . . .", *Ius est ecclesiae . . .* (Canon 807)

One wonders if our speech would not be more ecumenical (in the broadest sense of the term) if the canon stated "The church is ready to offer the service of establishing and directing universities . . .

While it made good sense for the church to claim its own rights in an officially Christian state (or in Christendom); it is hardly a suitable way of approaching a modern secularist society.

Practical consequences

Some important practical consequences flow from the proposed understanding of Catholic universities:

*To begin with, this understanding transfers the issue of "what a Catholic university is" from the abstract conceptual order (where the question is mostly handled and answered) into the concrete existential order. Now this should not be interpreted as denying the value of construing pure theories; they can be useful as far as they list "conceivable options"; what they cannot do, however, is to determine what option is the best for a given place at a given time. Thus, a theory may well set the ideal structures for a Catholic university, but in practice those structures may not be in harmony with the traditions of a culture (no culture is perfect), or may even be in plain conflict with the local laws; hence to impose and enforce them would defeat the very purposes of a Catholic university.

*Further, it cautions about universal legislation that would impose one pattern in differing situations. A law conceived on the basis of a theory may not only fail to promote the desired values but may even destroy the values which are being promoted. Since we live in an imperfect world, a perfect law can be destructive of the only obtainable values.[14]

---

[14]In our age, in an increasing number of countries, the church is existing and operating in conditions which it has perhaps never experienced in its

*Also, the shifting of the problem to the practical order could put an end to the endless and infertile discussions as to what the "essence" of a Catholic university is, and open the door to greater mutual understanding of different situations.

*Finally, it should bring home to all of us that at the final resort the Catholic orientation of a university rests on the judgment and decisions of persons, which cannot be made once for all. To maintain the Catholic character demands an ongoing dedication and alertness; "Catholic" structures may save appearances but not the substance if the persons are failing. In fact, the idea of Catholic

---

two thousand years of history: virtually total freedom in an indifferent state. In the pre-Constantine Roman empire it was (by and large) oppression in a religiously lukewarm state. Then it was freedom in close juridical association with the state (the age of Christendom: established church with rights and duties, various struggles between the two "perfect societies", etc.).

Canon law, as we have it today, is the product of the age of this latter type of relationship between church and state when it was necessary to vindicate and to define the rights of the church toward the secular authority—with which it was (sometimes for the better, sometimes for the worse) in permanent partnership. Hence the church claimed the right to property, to schools, to evangelize . . . and so forth. Ecclesiastical institutions had to be precisely defined canonically because otherwise their identity was not recognized by the state. E.g. there could not be a Catholic university without an ecclesiastical charter and jurisdictional ties. But how much canonical legislation is necessary in the new conditions? There is little experience to guide us. Is it too much to say that the church must learn how to define and guide its institutions in a climate of virtually unlimited freedom?

university which I offer is a very demanding one. It requires a commitment of all the constituencies not only to the usual academic ideals but also to ideals known by faith alone. Moreover, because it is not satisfied with the establishment of static structures but requires an internal dynamism to keep the religious orientation alive and developing, it genuinely speaks of a living Catholic institution.

Let me add also that the solution I offer has nothing to do with an existential philosophy that builds its positions out of the shifting sand of circumstances. My thoughts are grounded in an authentic metaphysical system, rooted in Aristotle and Aquinas, both of whom hold fast to the principle that values, that is, "what is good" for a concrete living being, exist in the concrete order only.

Bond of communion, bond of law

I wish now to return to the "types" for more comments on them.

The six could be further reduced to three categories:

* the first and second are not Catholic in the proper sense of the term;

* the third and fourth build their relationship on some kind of communion with the Catholic community;

* the fifth and sixth are legally incorporated into the canonical structures of the church.

No more needs to be said about the first group that professes no bond with the church. The two others need our attention. They represent two types of association with the church, the one is through communion, the other is through legal incorporation.

Before we go any further, let me give some background to these two concepts. Communion, or *koinonia* in Greek and *communio* in Latin, was a most powerful source of strength and action in the early church at a time when there were no significant legal structures and virtually no central organization. It was a firm dedication to unity, which inspired appropriate actions on the part of all, bishops and faithful. This happened at a time when the church displayed extraordinary energies and kept expanding into the whole known world. Now, if this communion could have been such a powerful factor in holding the church together in ancient times, surely it can be strong enough to hold a university and the believing community together in modern times.

From the twelfth century onwards, in the Western church, powerful legal structures began to develop. They became particularly helpful in unifying the church and directing its activities in the counter-reformation period, which lasted from the sixteenth into the twentieth century. They did more, however: they caused a shift in the Catholic mind. Both the hierarchy and the faithful gradually attributed increasing importance to laws in preserving the unity of the church.[15] The steady expansion of a centralized administration is a result of this mentality. Vatican Council II laid the theological foundations for the reversal of the trend, and the authorities in the church have taken important steps toward promoting decentralization. At the same time, undeniably, new efforts toward increased centralization appeared as well.[16]

[15]The Council of Trent, without ever intending it, had put the church on a course where "legal correctness" increasingly overshadowed some greater values. The Council created the idea of "legal authenticity"; for instance, it declared the Latin translation of the Scriptures known as the Vulgate the "authentic" text, to be used in all instructions and disputations; there followed the neglect of the original and inspired text. The popes after the Council declared that the "authentic" meaning of the Council can be given by the Holy See only and forbade access to the original acts; there followed an ignorance of what happened and a reliance for the true meaning of a text on an authoritative ("jurisdictional") pronouncement.

Such procedures led to the development of a mentality which gave an overriding importance to legislation and jurisdictional acts, but felt little need to return to the original sources.

[16]In our post-Vatican II church there is a great deal of *de iure* decentralization, but there is also a steadily increasing amount of *de facto* centralization. This *de facto* centralization is manifest when, e.g., the episcopal conferences can approve certain liturgical rites (they have the power in law) but only after Rome has reviewed the issue (they must not do so unless authorized to act); the chancellor of an ecclesiastical faculty has the right to grant tenure but he must not do so until he has received a *nihil obstat* from Rome. Also, there is a steady stream of instructions to bishops and others directing them how to "use their judgment" when by law they would be free, e.g. in the administration of the sacraments. It

The point I wish to make in connection with Catholic universities is that when their catholicity rests on communion with the church, the bond can be just as strong as if it rested on legal incorporation or jurisdictional ties. I assume, of course, that those who live by communion are determined to uphold it.[17]

would be difficult for an impartial theologian to argue that such developments are in the spirit of Vatican Council II.

[17]In this context I would like to draw attention to a development in the history of Catholic universities in the United States, a development which is of greatest importance and to date has not been sufficiently noted.

I am thinking of the extraordinary service and accomplishment of numerous boards of trustees in majority composed of lay persons. They have been in operation in many universities for about fifteen years or so.

The lay trustees have demonstrated their dedication to Catholic ideals. They have worked with the clergy, presided over them at the meetings of the boards, with much satisfaction on both sides. Lay persons have assumed the lion's share in financial management, and demonstrated a sense of responsibility which invites nothing but admiration.

In the board rooms of universities a silent revolution has taken place and keeps proving itself. Lay persons can take responsibility for Catholic institutions, they can preside over the members of the clergy, and with them, participate in decisions taken by the majority. The clerical members of the board and of the administration of the university are finding no difficulty in reporting and accounting to them. No complaint has been heard (certainly not by this writer) that any lay trustee would have sought to exercise undue influence over religious matters through his or her financial power.

Such a silent revolution, which is an effective demonstration of the capacity and of the sense of responsibility of our laity, was possible because the universities where all this happened were not under ecclesiastical jurisdiction.

Such a determination is necessary also for those who abide by legal structures; if the religious dimension of an institution is not sustained by the doctrine of communion, a reference to its catholicity can be described with Paul's words only: it will sound like a noisy gong or a clanging cymbal.

Now we can turn our attention more specifically to the interplay between the teaching authority and the believing community—as it takes place at a Catholic university.

Bond of communion (Cf. the third and fourth types)

This section refers to Catholic universities which profess a bond of communion with the church but do not have a legal personality in canon law. Let me stress again that in itself such a bond of communion need not be any weaker than a relationship of legal incorporation, but it is of a different order. It is a bond of common beliefs, mutual trust and respect, revealing itself in practical support and help.

Our question now is: Assuming this bond of communion, what should the relationship be between the magisterium and the university (*as an institution*)?

I wonder what the significance of this development is for our parishes, dioceses, and even for the universal church; and above all for determining the role of the laity in the church.

Whatever it is, it cannot be a legal relationship because there is no specific superior-to-subject relationship between the teaching authority and the university. There is, however, another bond that has its own binding force on a different level. If the university is committed to Catholic beliefs, it needs to hold in respect whatever the magisterium may declare for the whole church; otherwise how could it be so committed?! But such an act of respect (shall I call it *obsequium*?) will spring from a spontaneous dedication, not from any legally enforceable obligation. As always, this *obsequium* ought to be given according to the particular weight and authority of the declaration, as I explained above.

In fact, the response of a Catholic university to a magisterial pronouncement can be greatly helpful in two ways: the university can strengthen the position of the church by its respect for the declaration; or it can contribute to further research if the proclamation is a step toward the whole truth but as yet is not a conclusive judgment.

Examples can be given: if the church strongly condemns racial discrimination, a university which professes to be in communion with the church, must not preach or practice such a discrimination. Or, if the church strongly promotes human rights, the university can do much to support such a movement. If the magisterium issues a provisional judgment on a question of bioethics, continued research at universities could contribute out of their own resources toward the further refining of that judgment.[18]

Such an exchange between the magisterium and the university can lead to great enrichment for both sides, and can benefit the whole church. But it can work only in a climate of mutual respect and trust.

Problems, however, could occur. For instance, those who participate in the magisterium (the Congregation for the Doctrine of the Faith, the bishop of the diocese) could conceive their relationship to the university as a juridical one, and proceed accordingly, by issuing an order to be obeyed. But such an approach, if it ever happened, would be based on a misunderstanding. In the correct perception of the relationship, the task of the magisterium *toward the insitution* is to enlighten and to support, to encourage and to inspire, and not to issue legal precepts.

The task of the university is to be responsive, out of the strength of its original dedication. Such an exchange can become a fine and fruitful play. Admittedly, from time to time it can be spoiled by human elements, ill-conceived responses and delays; but that too is part of the bond of

[18]Whenever a declaration by the magisterium is based on the natural law, further contribution and help from universities can be vitally important. Since the church has never canonized a philosophical system, in the case of a particular instruction based on philosophical principles, the issue cannot be closed since infallibility cannot be invoked. Responsible scholarly work will be more needed than ever, especially when the issue directly touches the lives of people.

communion among human institutions. With the best of intentions, distrust and impatience may arise on either side. If there is, however, enough confidence in the internal strength of the Word that both sides believe in and honor, misunderstandings and conflicts should eventually be resolved in harmony.

But what if dissent arises within the university on the part of an individual Catholic teacher? Then we have to distinguish between the relationship of the hierarchy to that teacher, and its relationship to the university. As canon law is now, the matter must be handled between the competent ecclesiastical authority and the teacher.

The new Code of Canon Law has a legal provision in canon 812, which must serve as a guide. It prescribes that

> They who teach theological disciplines in any kind of institutes of higher studies must have the mandate of the competent ecclesiastical authority.[19]

Undoubtedly, the rule of mandate, confers a significant legal power on "the competent ecclesiastical authority," the

---

[19] I broke up the text to facilitate its understanding; the translation is my own. Here is the Latin original:

> *Qui in studiorum superiorum institutis quibuslibet disciplinas tradunt theologicas, auctoritatis ecclesiasticae competentis mandatum habeant oportet.*

The text allows no other construction than "They who teach, must . . .''; that is, the individual teacher has the obligation to obtain the mandate; it is a personal duty.

local ordinary in the first place, the Holy See on a higher level. They can grant to someone the right to teach, or they can deny it or withdraw it. They can certainly set up norms for each of these acts. Precisely because this power is so significant, no effort should be spared to understand it correctly.

The very opening words of the canon make it clear that the obligation is imposed on individual persons who intend to teach any of the theological disciplines; it does not go any further. No other interpretation is compatible with the text, and the general norms for interpretation forbid extending the burden, *onus,* any further than the law extends it.[20] Thus, there is no legal duty imposed on the institution.

[20]*A canonical query:* Could an ecclesiastical authority (the Holy See or the local ordinary) invoke canon 812 and order a Catholic university which has no legal personality in canon law to appoint as teachers of theology only those who have obtained the mandate?

The response cannot be but negative. The reason is twofold: (1) no ecclesiastical authority has the right to impose a duty on an institution which is non-existent in canon law; (2) no institution can be bound to accept an order from an office which has no jurisdiction over it as an institution. Indeed, I cannot think of an ecclesiastical court that would uphold and enforce such an order.

It may be argued, however, that universities *chartered by the Holy See* have an indirect legal obligation to give effect to this canon in its hiring policies, precisely because they already operate in the framework of canon law; therefore they cannot ignore a canonical provision. The same arguments could not be used in the case of Catholic universities which are related to the church through the bond of communion, because they do not operate in the framework of canon law.

Let us turn now from the textual exegesis to a practical example. Let us suppose that a teacher, Catholic and entrusted with the teaching of Catholic theology, deviates from the Catholic doctrine in a substantial manner; he declares himself publicly as a follower of Arius (c. 250-336, heresiarch), he claims that the *Logos* was created, *factum non genitum,* and he professes himself a dissenter from the doctrine of the Council of Nicaea. Surely a heretic by the standard of most Christian communities. (Of course, more modern examples could be adduced; but none clearer than this one.)

The magisterium would be acting within its competence, if it recalled the profession of faith of Nicaea and declared that the belief embraced by the teacher is contrary to the Catholic faith. It could certainly state that a person holding such views does not belong to the believing community. That much should settle the problem between the church and the newly born Arian. If he had a mandate, it should be withdrawn.

But what about the university? Should it take notice of the situation and proceed to action? Most certainly it should take notice of all the factors in the case, and then, through its appropriate procedures, form its own prudential judgment of what the proper action should be. The available options may depend on the local conditions, some circumstances being beyond the control of the university. For instance, it may well be that the laws of the country would protect the vested right of the heretical teacher to tenure, in fact, they would compel the university to continue his employment. If so, it would be imprudent for the university to enter into a litigation that it could not win. The sensible option would be to reinforce its theology department in such a way that the Nicean doctrine is clearly stated, and the inconsistency of the opposite view with the whole of Christian tradition demonstrated.

It would be a mistake to think that the best way of training students consists always in protecting them from erroneous views. Even if such protection worked at the university, they would encounter them as soon as they exit from their sheltered environment, if there is a sheltered environment at any university today! At times, to witness a real conflict while at school may be more formative than many lectures.

Bond of communion and of law
(Cf. the fifth and sixth types.)

When a university obtains a charter form the Holy See, it enters into the legal world of the church and becomes part of its structures and operations. Literally a host of new legal relations arise because a new juridic person has been created. Such a university, as an institution, is bound by all the ecclesiastical laws applicable to it; it is subject to the supervision of the appropriate offices of the Holy See and to the local bishop, both of whom have over it the *potestas regiminis,* the power to govern (although in different measures); to them the university must account with regularity.

Moreover (this is rarely realized) the university by becoming a juridic person in the church, may enter into another cultural world as well. Since the church is human, and universities are of human creation, there may be differences in the very conception of what a university is or ought to be. Such things do not surface at the joyful moments of the foundation but at the difficult times of the implementation.

Further, if the same university is civilly chartered in its country, it will be under two legal systems, which may not operate in harmony. Practical cases may end up with no resolution, or better, with conflicting claims originating in different legal systems. Then, all the wisdom of Solomon may not be enough to find an equitable solution.

As we recall, the canonically chartered universities divide into two groups, "Catholic universities" and "Ecclesiastical faculties and universities," the former being closer to a genuine *universitas studiorum,* the latter specializing in research and instruction in "sacred sciences." Accordingly, there can be differences in the way the magisterium relates to them.

The "Catholic universities" (with an ecclesiastical charter; known also as "pontifical") have an indirect *legal* obligation to pay attention to canon 812 concerning the "mandate" because they are inserted into legal structures of the church. Their obligation is indirect because the duty of having the mandate is directly imposed on the individual teacher. But to be a legal person in the church, as these universities are, means that they must respect and uphold the internal legal order in the church which requires that a teacher should have the mandate. It follows that they have the right and duty to ascertain that the canonical requirements in their teachers are fulfilled.

I am somewhat cautious, however, because even such universities are embedded in a culture and may be functioning civilly on the strength of a legal system which does not allow the application of canon 812; at least not without putting the university into a disadvantaged position among others, such as loss of accreditation, public support, and so forth. If that is the case, the virtue of justice postulates the invocation of *epieikeia* in place of the straightforward application of the law.[21]

---

[21]According to Aristotle laws are in the service of the virtue of justice. But laws are by their nature limited; in some cases not only may they fail to do justice, they may even work injustice. The reason for this limitation is that all laws are general, abstract and impersonal, but all cases crying for justice are particular, concrete and personal. Therefore a corrective is needed if justice is to be done. This corrective is what he called *epieikeia*, often translated as equity; it is an exception to the law for the sake of true justice. (See *Nichomachean Ethics*, 5, 9.)

Since the need for a corrective flows from the very nature of law,

The "Ecclesiastical universities and faculties" have their own particular law in the Apostolic Constitution *Sapientia christiana*, and in the attached *Ordinationes*. Their overall purpose, however, is stated in the Code, in canon 815; it should be quoted in full because it is a difficult text.

> The church, on the strength of its mission to proclaim the truth, has the right to establish universities or ecclesiastical faculties, for the purposes of conducting research in sacred disciplines and in others connected with them; also for giving scientific instructions in the same disciplines.

The meaning of "church" is ambivalent: does it mean the community of all believers in a general way, or does it mean specifically the hierarchy? Surely, the whole church has the mission to proclaim the truth; yet in the context there can be no doubt that the word means the hierarchy.

Now the prime mission of the hierarchy is not to do scientific research, nor is it to give academic instruction, but to witness to God's mighty deeds. It follows that in such "pontifical faculties" a very delicate situation is created: the mission of witnessing is brought together with the task of the *academia*. Add to this that these "faculties" are usually instrumental in training candidates for ordination, which is a "sacrament of sending," and you can see

canonical norms may be in need of a corrective too. Should such a need emerge, it is legitimate to invoke *epieikeia*.

that the potential is there for conflicts between two perfectly legitimate but different orientations.[22]

The role of the magisterium in such institutions is reinforced by the requirements of the *missio canonica* (canonical mission), *venia docendi* (permission to teach), and *nihil obstat* (no objection), each of these applicable to a distinct group of teachers. Those who teach "disciplines of faith and morals" must have the mission before they can function; those who teach other subjects within the institution must have the permission, and those who are to be promoted to the highest academic rank (ordinary or full professor) or are to be tenured (at whatever rank) must have the "no objection." These requirements are more far-reaching than that of the mandate; the Constitution leaves no doubt that both the institution and the individual persons are bound by its norms.

The **canonical mission** is granted by the chancellor; he is usually the local ordinary but *as chancellor* he is also the representative of the Holy See toward the institution. The canonical mission is not unique to the academic world; for instance, bishops need it to take possession of their

---

[22]At the last count, the potential for conflict is, of course, not in the different tasks, witnessing and researching, but in human beings who are never omniscient and omnipotent. A theologian may be far ahead of a bishop in his insights into the mysteries; or a bishop may have a clearer and firmer perception of a mystery than a theologian for whom it is an object of analysis. The potential for conflict is in human beings.

diocese.[23] Literally translated, it means an official sending, or a lawful commissioning. In practice it is the act by which an office is definitely conferred. It is the final confirmation of the appointment on the part of an ecclesiastical authority, no matter in what way the candidate arrived at the threshold of that position, by way of an election, through a nomination, or as the result of a promotion.[24]

Although the canonical mission presupposes manifold qualifications, scientific and educational, ultimately it is

[23]The meaning and scope of the canonical mission, however, is not the same in the case of a bishop as in the case of a teacher.

The bishop receives his canonical mission from the pope; he is assigned a portion of the people of God for his pastoral care; he is inserted into the visible and hierarchical structure of the church; he obtains legislative, judicial and executive power over his diocese. (In a now antiquated perception, he received the power of jurisdiction over the diocese.)

The teacher receives a license to practice what he is professionally qualified for.

It would be better to reserve the expression "canonical mission" for bishops, and return to the traditional term "license" for teachers.

[24]The canonical mission can be granted explicitly or implicitly. Cf. LG 24:

> The canonical mission of bishops can come about by legitimate customs which have not been revoked by the supreme and universal authority of the Church, or by laws made or recognized by that same authority, or directly through the successor of Peter himself.

If it can be given implicitly to bishops, *a fortiori* it can be so given to teachers.

granted on the basis of a judgment on the religious suitability of the candidate. Such a grant, of course, can never make a bad theologian into a good one; it is the duty of the one who makes the grant to ascertain that the candidate is academically qualified.

Sapientia christiana gives the reason for the requirement of the canonical mission: "they do not teach by their own authority, but on the strength of a mission received from the church" (Art. 27 # 1). The correct interpretation of this clause is difficult. At times one hears it paraphrased as "they do not teach in their own name but in the name of the church," which, if anything, makes an explanation even more difficult.

Before anything else, there is again the problem with the term "church"; does it mean the whole church or does it mean the hierarchy? It cannot possibly mean the whole church (that is, the whole people of God!); the word must have a more limited sense. But it cannot mean the hierarchy either, at least not without some reservations. The episcopal power of witnessing the message is certainly not transferred by the canonical mission nor do the teachers acquire a charism to speak in the name of the church—as is given by the Spirit to the episcopal college. So what is the meaning of this "teaching on the strength of a mission (authority) received from the church"?

For an answer one must begin with the obvious question: what is given to a teacher by the canonical mission which he did not have before? It cannot be anything in the order of grace, or in the order of science, since the conferral of the canonical mission does not make anyone holier or more learned than he was before. It can only be something in the juridical order: it must be the approval for the office. The person becomes legally qualified to teach at an "ecclesiastical faculty."

By what authority then does the teacher teach? He certainly has the authority conferred on every Christian by baptism to proclaim the evangelical message. He is also invested with the authority to conduct courses, give lectures, carry out examinations, and participate in the government of the institution. As regards the content of his doctrine, it will have as much authority as the reasons supporting it; both Gratian and Aquinas would agree to that. Therefore, there is no magical change when a person is granted the canonical mission, either in his doctrinal authority or in his capacity as teacher; all that happens is that he can practice his profession at an ecclesiastical institution, in a position of trust.[25]

---

[25]It is interesting to compare the conception of Gratian and Aquinas with that of *Sapientia christiana* concerning the authority by which a magister teaches. Neither of the two medieval authors speaks of the authority of the church being somehow vested in the teacher; both make it clear that the authority a teacher must invoke is that of reason (meaning reason informed and enlightened by faith). The implication is that the teacher's doctrine has authority as far as it is supported by reason. True, Aquinas insists that a license is required for teaching, but it does not occur

Thus, the meaning of the clause quoted can be rendered as "teachers in an ecclesiastical faculty do not have their position on their own authority but through an appointment (or the approval of it) from the competent ecclesiastical superior," which is plain English, correct theology and makes good sense.[26]

to him that such a juridical act could give any authority to the doctrine taught.

Sapientia christiana seems to imply that by the fact that the magister teaches "on the strength of a mission received from the church" his doctrine somehow obtains greater authority. This may be true of episcopal teaching in appropriate circumstances; it cannot be true of academic teaching, which must be based on the authority of reason—as explained.

An interesting study would be how the sharp medieval distinction between the two types of teaching has become somewhat obliterated. One historical reason might well be found in the sad state of theology after the Council of Trent when disputed issues about the Council (and indeed about the Scriptures) could not be resolved by turning to the original sources but had to be settled by a decree of the Congregation of the Council. A new concept developed: teaching with authority did not mean the invoking of reasons but the invoking of administrative decrees.

[26]Here we have another illustration of how difficult it is to get to the correct meaning of a text if the term "church" is not used with precision. Church means "gathering," *ecclesia*; it means the whole of it. The so-called "clericalization" of the church was a regrettable historical development; it caused a shift in the understanding of the word "church." If by some kind of holy conspiracy all the theologians and canon lawyers agreed to use the term "church" only in its true sense, that is, in reference to the whole *ecclesia*, they would be doing a great service to the whole community. Gradually, all would become aware that when a document or decree (less than infallible) is published, it is the act of a Congregation, of an episcopal conference, of a particular bishop, but not "of the church." Without much explanation, believers and unbelievers would have a better knowledge of

The difference between the *cathedra pastoralis* (the authority of the bishop is rooted in his sacramental office), and the *cathedra magistralis* (the authority of the teacher is as good as his reasons) remains intact.[27]

The **permission to teach** is necessary for all other teachers within an ecclesiastical faculty; no matter what they teach; whether they are Catholics or not. The chancellor has the right to grant it.

The requirement of the **"no objection"** guarantees that no one will reach the highest rank or will get tenure if the Holy See, which alone is competent to issue the declaration, is not satisfied with the qualifications of the person. The procedure must be described in the statutes of each institution; the general law does not give further details.[28]

what the church is or is not, what it says or says not, what it does or does not. Of course, this moderate use would in no way prohibit one from saying "the church has spoken through the Council of Nicaea", or "the church must work for peace"—and so forth. The use is correct as long as it refers to an organ which can speak for the whole community or refers to the aspirations of all.

[27]Undoubtedly, the close association between the episcopal authority and the teaching function at an ecclesiastical faculty can lead to unwarranted transfers: the hierarchy may expect the teachers simply to echo their statements (they teach in the name of the church!), or the teachers may proclaim their opinions without supporting them with valid reasons (thinking that they have a special authority).

[28]A complex process which may easily become lengthy beyond measure should any problem arise.

The surprising feature of this law is that even when there is a significant number of bishops directing and controlling the institution, they are not

Academic freedom

My purpose is not to give a full systematic exposition of the doctrine of academic freedom and of the problems connected with it; nor is it to propose precise practical rules for its protection. Such a vast enterprise would be well beyond the scope of this inquiry.

I intend to present the issue in fairly general terms, first by outlining its context, then by identifying its basic elements, finally by outlining some practical rules which can be helpful for the protection of this freedom.

What is the context? The broad context is indicated by the very purpose of the university: to be the house of intellect in the community at large. A university is not an isolated self-serving institution; it exists for the sake of the society surrounding it. That society has created the university and keeps supporting it and renewing it by the influx of persons and funds. The university, in its turn, nourishes the community with knowledge and provides trained persons for all kinds of jobs and tasks. Its operations touch somehow the life of many (all?) of those who live and work outside its boundaries.

It follows that the issue of academic freedom is not merely an internal problem, to be left to and handled by the academicians alone. All those who have an interest in

authorized to make a judgment on the suitability of the candidate for promotion until the reception of the *nihil obstat* from Rome.

the university, have also an interest in academic freedom.

What is academic freedom? Let us begin with the general concept of freedom in an organized human society. The life of such a society turns on a balanced play between contrasting forces and interests. One of such a pair of forces is in the right-and-duty situations: if I have the right to a service, someone somewhere has the duty to perform it. Another one is in the freedom-and-restraint situations; if I have the freedom to speak, all others are restrained from interfering with it. Those who have a freedom are like persons living in a protected territory; the others are enjoined from entering it.

In the case of academic freedom the territory in question is the *academia.* Those who belong to it are entitled to carry out their activities unhampered. Such activities are manifold; the most prominent among them are those which are directly connected with the primary purpose of the university, such as gathering information, proposing insights, testing hypotheses, formulating judgments (probable or certain), communicating knowledge to others, and so forth. Other operations too postulate freedom: the testing of the students, participation in the government of the institution, as well as serving the general public in an intellectual way through lecturing and publishing.

All considered, academic freedom is nothing else than the freedom to do what is necessary to help the university to fulfill its purpose. Clearly any community which wants a university in its midst wants academic freedom as well; which is to say that it wants to restrain the citizens from interfering with the *academia*.

How can academic freedom be assured? The problem is not a new one; it must have surfaced in the middle ages, otherwise it would be difficult to explain why the *universitates studiorum* were constantly seeking exemption from local jurisdiction, ecclesiastical and civil, and wished to place themselves under the protection of popes and emperors. Such efforts clearly show a realization that the house of intellect serves a broad human purpose which transcends the local interests. Inside the universities, new institutions sprouted from this conception of freedom, such as internal and autonomous courts of justice, elected representatives to be sent to the parliament, and others.

To this day in some European countries academic freedom is assured by constitutional provisions, not unlike the independence of judges. In the United States accrediting agencies, professional societies, and departments of education of individual states and courts of law, all contribute, each in its own way, to the safeguarding of academic freedom.

In the church, the new Code of Canon Law, lists among the fundamental rights of the faithful the freedom of inquiry:

> Those who are engaged in the study of sacred disciplines, in matters in which they are experts, enjoy the just freedom of inquiry and of expressing their mind prudently, with due *obsequium* toward the magisterium of the church. (Canon 218)

This canon is applicable to anyone who is engaged in the study of, say, theology; but the prime place for its application is obviously within the boundaries of the Catholic universities and ecclesiastical faculties. It is reinforced by another one:

> The faithful are entitled to vindicate and defend lawfully their rights, which they enjoy in the church, before a competent ecclesiastical forum, according to the norm of the law. (Canon 221 § 1)[29]

What are the limits of academic freedom? Freedom in an organized society always has its limits since it imposes a restraint on others; unlimited freedom would mean unlimited restraint. The limits in our case are determined by the boundaries of the *academia;* nothing more, nothing less. As long as the reflecting, teaching, communicating is in the service of the purpose of the house of intellect,

---

[29]Unfortunately the provisions of canon law for all practical purposes end there. I say for practical purposes because although theoretically there are ways and means of vindicating rights in the church, in the practical order the procedures are most of the time so complex, protracted and expensive, that a thoughtful canon lawyer will hardly ever counsel someone to initiate such a case.

freedom is justified. If someone uses his position at a university for the promotion of other causes, such as for the spreading of unscientific ideologies or the support of commercial interests, he is surely overstepping the legitimate boundaries of freedom.

Can religious principles set limits to academic freedom? The answer depends on the nature of the university. In a secular university operating in a pluralistic society it would be utterly wrong to set a limit on the basis of religious ideas. This is so clear that I do not see any need to discuss it further.

But if the constituencies of a university have freely chosen to commit themselves to the service of religious values, the situation is different. They have exercised their freedom by adding this specific scope to the generally recognized purpose of the university. If they want to operate within that scope, they must have permanent freedom to direct their operations toward it, and to demand that others should be restrained from interfering with it. If not, the commitment to those values is worthless.

It follows, of course, that a person who is unwilling to accept or respect the choice for religious values, should never participate in the work of an institution so committed. This is simply a matter of fairness and honesty for all concerned.

But human nature being what it is, problems still may arise. There could be misunderstandings in the beginning.

There could be even a change of heart in someone; a person may not wish to support or even to respect values that at one time he had judged desirable; in fact he may undertake a campaign against the same values right at the university. What to do then?

The ideal solution would be in a peaceful separation, which is usually the most efficient way of preserving respect for each other. If that is not possible, the next course of action depends on the local circumstances.

If the university is civilly chartered but has no canonical status, the matter ought to be regulated according to civil law. For the rest, it should be a matter for the wisdom of the university to find a way of safeguarding its own dedication—with fairness to all concerned.

If the university is merely canonically chartered (there are such universities in Europe), the case will have to be handled within the framework of canon law, which, as we have seen, provides in various ways for the protection of the Catholic orientation of the institution (cf. the requirement of mandate, canonical mission, etc.).[30]

If the university is both civilly and canonically chartered, there may well be a conflict of laws. Such a conflict is

---

[30]All judgment should operate within a sound hierarchy of values. An attempt to dismiss a teacher for proven opposition to the religious commitment of the university may result in the university losing its civil privileges and eventually losing its students as well. A strong and healthy institution should know how to create the necessary dialectics to clarify the situation; by dialectics I mean sound and vigorous academic debates.

hardly ever amenable to a resolution by principles because it originates in concrete and particular regulations. No one but those who are experts in both systems can even attempt to disentangle the complications. These are the situations to which I have already referred by saying that all the wisdom of Solomon may not be enough to find the *correct* solution. The *available* solution may be no more than an honest settlement among conflicting claims.[31]

Admittedly, the most delicate and complex cases are likely to arise in "ecclesiastical faculties" dedicated to research and teaching in sacred sciences. There freedom must be maintained within the parameters set by religious beliefs. Some guidelines and norms for achieving harmony can certainly be conceived, such as:

—the rights and duties of the individual faculty members and of the university should be clearly spelled out before any appointment is finalized;

—there should be good and workable structures to handle disputes or conflicts;

—besides the local remedies, there should always be ways and means for appeal.

Once these provisions are in place, it remains still true that there is no substitute for wisdom and prudence in all concerned. Even the best of structures can be turned into instruments of oppression or endless turmoil if they fall into the hands of the wrong persons.

[31]The Declaration on Religious Freedom of Vatican Council II undoubtedly has relevance for an understanding of a religiously committed university in a pluralistic society. The church must respect the mind of the nation (the light, imperfect as it may be, of the conscience of the nation) in organizing its own institutions of higher education; it cannot simply withdraw from the scene and follow its own ways. (*Dignitatis humanae*)

Who should be the judges? The right to judge belongs to
those who have responsibilities for, or towards, the
university. Accordingly, whatever the procedures may be,
they are likely to be complex. A good judicial system will
always try to give a scope to the intimate knowledge of the
insiders, and a scope to the detached perception of the
outsiders. Should there be a prima facie case of violation
(someone inside the university overstepping the boundaries, someone from the outside unduly interfering) it is
fair and just that those who are closest to the case and
know the circumstances best should form a first judgment;
this is the judgment of peers. It is equally fair and just that
there should be an opportunity for some kind of appeal, be
it to a constitutional court, or to an accrediting body, or to a
commission appointed for the purpose.

A remark concerning canonically chartered institutions. It is
now easy to locate the specific problem of ecclesiastically
chartered institutions: they are supervised by the episcopate
of which the specific task is pastoral care, and they have to
function as universities of which the scope is scientific
research and teaching.

The first step toward handling the relationship is the
awareness of this difference on both sides; otherwise, the
wrong types of expectations will build up. The hierarchy
will expect and request pastoral help; the researchers will
demand episcopal endorsement for their tentative hypotheses.

The second step is in balancing the proximity brought about by the bond of law with the due distance postulated by the differences in scope and task. Thus we come to say it again: ultimately it will be a matter for prudential judgment. No matter how perfect the statutes may be, how many rules are drawn up, there comes a point where there is no substitute for a sound particular judgment. To illustrate this, let me turn to the *magistra vitae*, history.

Lean years, rich years

Let me begin by narrating what happens if there is too much control. The story is not invented; it is history, from within living memory.

After the silences and privations imposed by the second World War, there was a sudden blossoming out of theological research and reflection in the Roman Catholic church, heralding the advent (or so it was thought) of a new theology. In reality, it was not all that new; its roots went back to various biblical, patristic and historical studies carried out (with interruptions and impediments) ever since the beginning of the century. Now, as happens always when there is a true effort to reach the truth, there were exaggerations and mistakes; but on the whole the fields were heavy with the promise of a rich harvest. Then, in 1950 the encyclical *Humani generis* was published, and in the wake of it (even if it was not so intended by the document) "the disciplining" of theologians began. Books were withdrawn from circulation, translations and new editions of "potentially harmful" works were forbidden (among them such a judicious one as Congar's *True and False Reform of the Church*). Some thinkers (Karl Rahner, John Courtney Murray) were ordered to submit their writings to special censorship. Well-known teachers were removed from their chairs, or restricted in some other way. What was the result?

In well-known and respectable theological schools a new climate developed. Some professors (the more creative ones) refused to publish their lectures or to put their thoughts into writing, for fear of being condemned. If someone wanted to know their doctrine, he had to go to "students' notes." Stenciled texts travelled from one place to another; I myself remember that when I was studying theology at Louvain (1948-52), some of Teilhard's (and of others') writings reached us in this way. Teachers tended to develop a new phraseology that both conveyed their ideas to the initiated and covered it up for all others. The subtle oppression did not really put an end to original thinking (or to the mistakes that accompanied it) but succeeded in creating a climate of distrust and suspicion.

It was a climate totally unbefitting the church of Christ. Fortunately Vatican Council II swept it away, and we have seen (I have seen), not without amazement, several of the theologians who not so long before were "under a cloud" present in Rome and advising the Fathers and helping them to draft the documents by which the church lives today.

If there is a lesson in this experience, it is that well-meant condemnations in the interest of truth can create a climate which is destructive for the truth. Then the second evil is worse than the first.

In ordinary circumstances, the church is strong and healthy enough to throw out the chaff, even if the process takes some time. The parable of the zealous servants is as valid as ever: premature weeding may well uproot the wheat. Besides, according to the same parable, the master knows about the conditions of his field, and has every intention to take care of it once the time has come for the harvest.

But this is not the note on which I wish to close this chapter: truth and fairness demand more.

The contribution of Catholic universities (of whatever type) to the progress of religion and culture is well known, no need to insist on it. The more specific achievement of "ecclesiastical universities and faculties" dedicated to "sacred sciences" is less known to the general public and at times is not fully perceived by experts either. To say that Vatican Council II was prepared quietly and unobtrusively in such places would not be an exaggeration—it was prepared by nothing else than the standard and quality of research and teaching. The finest tools in theological investigations, such as the *Dictionnaire de théologie catholique, Lexikon für Theologie und Kirche,* and *New Catholic Encyclopedia* have been conceived, created and composed mostly by faculty from such institutions. In one way or another, the Roman College (which has become the Gregorian University of Rome), the *Ecole Biblique* in Jerusalem, the *Institut Catholique* in Paris left an indelible impact on Catholic theology. To this day, the scientific standards of many publications coming out from such ecclesiastical faculties in Belgium, France, Germany, Italy, Spain and other countries bear witness to a dedication to the most rigorous standards of scholarship.

This is not to deny that there are institutions which have never reached such a level, perhaps have never come anywhere near it. My intention in quoting the achievements of good years is rather to confirm once again that when right persons are around and they can work in a climate of freedom and trust, there is bound to be a rich harvest.[32]

---

[32] I like to direct the reader's attention to a recent publication which came to my attention too late to be inserted into the Bibliography: James John Annarelli, *Academic Freedom and Catholic Higher Education* (New York: Greenwood Press, 1987). The book contains ample and important documentation on the history and issue of academic freedom in Catholic institutions in the United States.

EPILOGUE

There are the paradoxes of the Christian community: it will remain forever a learning church because the depth and breadth of God's mysteries can never be known; it will remain forever a teaching church also because God's mighty deeds for our salvation must be proclaimed to the whole creation.

Further, its progress toward the fullness of the truth will be marked always by joy and frustration; it has never been easy for human beings to get acquainted and with divine mysteries. The twelve apostles could testify to that.

Perhaps there is no other activity in the church where the limitations of our human nature can be more strikingly revealed than in our efforts to advance toward the fullness of the truth. But weak as we are, we are not without hope; in our weakness the strength of God can become manifest.

The prayer of the Psalmist may be appropriate for all of us:

> May the Lord give strength to his people!
> May the Lord bless his people with peace!
> (Ps 29:11)

BIBLIOGRAPHY

Barzun, Jacques. *The House of Intellect.* New York: Harper & Row, 1959.

> A critical examination of the intellectual standards of our society and of our universities; neither comes out very well. Witty and insightful.

Bok, Derek. *Higher Learning.* Cambridge, MA: Harvard University Press, 1986.

> A description of the American higher educational system and a discussion of its problems by the President of Harvard.

Castelli, Enrico, ed. *L'infallibilité: son aspect philosophique et théologique.* Paris: Aubier, 1970.

> The acts of a congress held in Rome in 1970; the papers presented by 37 authors consider infallibility from many points of view: epistemological, psychological, religious, dogmatic, etc. They cover much more than the Catholic dogma.

Chirico, Peter. *Infallibility: The Crossroads of Doctrine.* Wilmington, DE: Glazier, 1985.

A reflective work; the author presents an original understanding of infallibility mainly on the basis of Lonergan's epistemology.

Congar, Yves. *Vrai et fausse réforme dans l'Eglise.* Second ed. revised and corrected. Paris: Cerf, 1968.

A classic in theological "wisdom literature". This edition contains a new Preface and a *Postface,* also an Appendix on *Responsabilité collective* and another on *Fidelité.*

Congar, Yves. *History of Theology.* Translated from the French. Garden City, NY: Doubleday, 1986.

A history of the science of theology.

Dulles, Avery. *Models of Revelation.* Garden City, NY: Image Books, 1985.

In the first part of the book five models are described and examined: Revelation as Doctrine, History, Inner Experience, Dialectical Presence and New Awareness; in the second part the author gives his own systematic explanation of revelation "as the self manifestation of God through a form of communication that could be termed, at least in a broad sense, symbolic" (p. 266).

Faivre, Alexandre. *Les laics aux origines de l'Eglise.* Paris: Le Centurion, 1984.

In the first five centuries lay persons not only served in important offices in the church but were able to shape its life in many ways. The author reflects on our problems today and asks what can we do to recover the best of our ancient traditions.

Faivre, Alexandre. *Naissance d'une hiérarchie.* Paris: Beauchesne, 1977.

> A detailed and thorough historical account of the emergence of the distinction between clergy and laity from the beginnings to the times of Pope Gregory the Great. It contains a most helpful classified bibliography.

Fransen, Piet F. *Hermeneutics of the Councils and Other Studies.* Leuven: University Press, 1985.

> A collection of ground-breaking essays; some are particularly enlightening about the interpretation of the Tridentine decrees.

Granfield, Patrick. *The Limits of the Papacy: Authority and Autonomy in the Church.* New York: Crossroad, 1987.

> The main themes of this book are: the development of the papal office, its possible limitations, the balance between the head and the members in the episcopal college, the relationship between the church of Rome and the local churches, the reception of papal teaching by the faithful, the papacy and the ecumenical movement. A historically well-grounded study with thoughtful and nuanced conclusions.

Gustafson, James M. *Treasure in Earthen Vessels: The Church as a Human Community.* Midway Reprint. Chicago: University of Chicago Press, 1976.

> A professor of Christian ethics reflects, in the form of a long essay, on the humanity of the church.

Hassel, David, J. *City of Wisdom: A Christian Vision of the American University*. Chicago: Loyola University Press, 1983.

A rather comprehensive work in two parts: "The University Takes Stock of Itself", and "The University Looks to Its Powers". It is well informed; on the issue of the Catholic university it presents well an ideal (or ideal models); at times one wonders how much the author is aware of many real problems (e.g., state interference; inability to assume responsibility for a religiously oriented climate among the students; declining financial resources, etc.).

Hertling, Ludwig. *Communio: Church and Papacy in Early Christianity*. Translated from the German (ed. 1962). Chicago: Loyola University Press, 1972.

A small study of exceptional and lasting value on the position of the See of Rome in the early church.

Kaplin, William A. *The Law of Higher Education: A Comprehensive Guide to Legal Implications of Administrative Decision Making*. Second ed. San Francisco: Jossey-Bass, 1985.

A comprehensive manual (or reference book) of the laws of higher education (federal and state) in the United States, conceived for administrators but equally useful for trustees, faculty, students and members of accrediting agencies who are interested in the legal aspects of college or university life.

Lagrange, M.-J. *Père Lagrange: Personal Reflections and Memoirs.* New York: Paulist Press, 1985. Translation from the French.

> A most instructive reading about the struggles with "the teaching office" of a pioneer in modern Catholic biblical scholarship.

Leff, Gordon. *Paris and Oxford Universities in the Thirteenth and Fourteenth Centuries.* New York: Wiley, 1968.

> A history of the two universities, describing their origins, structures, and giving much space to their intellectual development and influence.

Mühlen, Heribert. *Una mystica persona: Eine Person in vielen Personen.* Second revised ed. Paderborn: Ferdinand Schöningh, 1967.

> One of the finest works to appear after Vatican Council II on the theology of the church; unfortunately little known in the English-speaking countries. It is available also in French translation.

Newman, John Henry. *An Essay on the Development of Christian Doctrine.* Reprint. Garden City, NY: Doubleday, 1960.

> This is the work that for the first time gave an intelligent explanation of the development of doctrine in the Christian church. It has remained a classic; it had a strong impact on Vatican Council II, especially on the Constitution on Divine Revelation, *Dei verbum.*

Newman, John Henry. *The Idea of a University.* Reprint. Garden City, NY: Doubleday, 1959.

The idea that Newman was never allowed to put into practice. An ideal that remained an inspiration but was never fully incarnated in any university.

Page, Jean-Guy. *Qui est l'Eglise?* 3 vols. Montreal: Editions Bellarmin, 1977, 1979, 1979.

Although the author describes his work as a textbook for students and pastors, it is much more. It is a comprehensive treatise and a rich encyclopedia of ecclesiology, with abundant bibliographical references.

Pelikan, Jaroslav. *The Christian Tradition: A History of the Development of Doctrine.* 5 vols. Chicago: University of Chicago Press. 1971, 1974, 1978, 1984, 5th volume to be published.

A reflective history of how revelation was perceived by Christians in different ages; written from a great store of knowledge. Definitely not a first book either in historical or systematic theology.

Söll, Georg. *Dogma und Dogmenentwicklung.* Handbuch der Dogmengeschichte, Band I, Faszikel 5. Freiburg/BR: Herder, 1971.

The most up-to-date and comprehensive work on the history of the problem of the development of dogma.

Sullivan, Francis A. *Magisterium: Teaching Authority in the Catholic Church.* Mahwah, NJ: Paulist Press, 1983.

An explanation of the meaning of *magisterium*, a presentation of contemporary problems in a historical framework. A book written by a scholar for the public at large.

Thorndike, Linn. *University Records and Life in the Middle Ages.* Reprint. New York: Norton, 1973.

A collection of records kept by great medieval universitites such as Paris, Bologna, Heidelberg and others. A most interesting first-hand documentation about every facet of the life of the students and teachers.

Tillard, J-M.R. *The Bishop of Rome.* Translation from the French. Wilmington, DE: Glazier, 1983.

Highly informative, especially from a historical point of view.

Tillard, J-M.R. *Eglise d'églises: L'ecclésiologie de communion.* Paris: Cerf, 1987.

A historical and systematic treatise on the church, with all traditional themes present but presented and considered under the aspect of *communio.* A work of great erudition and of strong ecumenical inspiration.

Walgrave, Ian. *Unfolding Revelation: The Nature of Doctrinal Development.* Translation from the Dutch. Philadelphia: Westminster, 1972.

The best work available in English on the development of doctrine. A rich historical survey leads up to systematic discussions; the author's own conclusions are inspired by Newman.

Index

Index

ABOUT THE AUTHOR

Ladislas Örsy, S.J., is internationally respected as a leading expert in canon law. He has written several books and over 200 articles on canonical and theological questions. He holds his doctorate in canon law from the Gregorian University, took his degree in civil law from Oxford University, and did his graduate theological studies at Louvain University. He is presently on the faculty of The Catholic University of America.